CAMBRIDGESHIRE LANDSCAPE GUIDELINES

A MANUAL FOR MANAGEMENT AND CHANGE IN THE RURAL LANDSCAPE

Published by:
Cambridgeshire County Council
Shire Hall
Castle Hill
Cambridge CB3 0AP
in association with
Granta Editions, Cambridge

COUNTRYSIDE COMMISSION

with
Countryside Commission (Eastern Region)
East Cambridgeshire District Council
Fenland District Council
Huntingdonshire District Council
Peterborough City Council
South Cambridgeshire District Council
Cambridge City Council

Consultants:
Landscape Design Associates
17 Minster Precincts
Peterborough PE1 1XX

CAMBRIDGESHIRE LANDSCAPE GUIDELINES

A MANUAL FOR MANAGEMENT
AND CHANGE
IN THE RURAL LANDSCAPE

Published by
Cambridgeshire County Council
in association with
Granta Editions

© Cambridgeshire County Council 1991.

Published by Cambridgeshire County Council and
Granta Editions of 47 Norfolk Street, Cambridge
CB1 2LE.

Granta Editions is an imprint of The Book Concern
Limited.

A CIP catalogue record for this book is available from
the British Library.

ISBN 0 906782 74 0

Designed by Peter Dolton.

Design, editorial and production in association with
Book Production Consultants, 47 Norfolk Street,
Cambridge CB1 2LE.

Printed and bound by The Burlington Press, Foxton,
Cambridge.

Preface

A conference arranged by the Countryside
Commission at Spalding in May 1987 first
drew attention to the need for guidelines
for change in the Fenland landscapes. The
approach set out in this manual was
adopted as a policy proposal for the whole
of Cambridgeshire in the Rural Strategy,
published in May 1988.

We wish to see landscapes treated
positively as an integral part of the
development process and the husbandry of
rural land. The manual therefore offers
guidance to those groups of people who, in
their various ways, are now creating the
future landscape.

The manual was approved by the County
Council on 25 February 1991 and is now
offered for use as supplementary planning
guidance. We also commend it to everyone
who can, in some way, help to nurture or
recreate our highly valued local landscapes.

John P Reach

Chairman
Environmental Services Committee
Cambridgeshire County Council

June 1991

Acknowledgements

Grateful acknowledgement is due to the following:

– Landscape Design Associates whose report 'Cambridgeshire Landscape Guidelines' has provided the bulk of the source material, including the drawn illustrations;
– the Countryside Commission, who sponsored the 1987 Spalding Conference where the idea originated, and supported this project with advice and grant aid;
– the district councils of Cambridgeshire, who gave financial support, advice and guidance;
– the many consultees whose responses have helped refine the text and whose support adds to its authority;
– staff of the Property Department, with help from Corporate Planning, who developed this manual from the consultants' report;
– and Peter Lake who took the photographs.

RICHARD GOODALL
Director of Property
Cambridgeshire County Council

Contents

1

SHARE
THE
VISION

Landscape influences the quality of our working, travelling, domestic and recreational lives. It reflects the richness of our ecological and historic heritage. If we recognise this, we can develop and share a vision for tomorrow's landscape.

The vision which this manual invites you to share is of a countryside which is diverse, reflecting local character and a sense of place, consciously thought about and managed, and which acknowledges our affinity with nature and our need for recreation and visual enjoyment.

These landscape guidelines recognise the potential for everyone involved with the rural landscape and its settlements to play a part in achieving that vision. They will be of particular relevance to those who have the greatest influence on the landscape – farmers, developers and engineers, and public bodies.

A SAD DECLINE

During the post-war period, there have been dramatic changes in the Cambridgeshire landscape. Particularly in the 1980s, observers alerted us to the environmental decline of the countryside: critics felt that much of what was valued had been lost and much of what was new was bland, insensitive and lacking in character; the Cambridgeshire countryside

Looking east across the fens from Ely Cathedral's western tower.

With the kind permission of the Dean and Chapter.

of old had gone. This is true, in the sense that there is no going backwards, no way of fully restoring many of the lost habitats, and no prospect of doing away with intrusive new structures. Along with the loss of habitats we have seen the erosion of a sense of place and local character, those difficult-to-define features of the countryside which create a special local identity and may inspire creative thought or give pleasure to the resident and visitor alike.

TIME FOR CREATIVE RENEWAL

Some action has been taken to tackle these problems; central and local government, landowners and voluntary bodies have played a part. The tree planting programme in Cambridgeshire is one example.

But the opportunities which present themselves now are of a much greater magnitude. They arise from:

– the likelihood of major changes in farming, with the possibility that some land will no longer be needed for food production;

– continuing economic and population growth in the County;

– growing environmental awareness amongst the population at large; people are looking for better and more rewarding environments, both urban and rural, and for reassurance that we can live alongside nature.

These guidelines are therefore forward-looking and endeavour to offer creative inspiration. It is only through a vision of new standards that problems of implementation can be overcome. There will indeed be problems: some will argue that agricultural economics are still ill-disposed to the planting of trees and

woodlands; development economics may discourage high design standards or innovations with landscape creation; engineering standards and financial constraints reduce the scope for achieving environmentally sensitive road schemes; local authorities have reduced budgets, and so on. A clearer vision should help to overcome these constraining factors.

Decades of decline, at the approach to St Neots from the east.

The landscape guidelines for Cambridgeshire describe a series of ways in which new, richer and more diverse landscapes can be developed. Just as small detrimental changes cumulatively damage a landscape, so can small creative actions improve it, and develop a new character. The guidelines illustrate how farmers, developers (and their architects), engineers, local authorities, conservation volunteers, landscape professionals and the general public can contribute towards this objective.

2

ACCEPT
THE
CHALLENGE

OBJECTIVES FOR LANDSCAPE RENEWAL

The creative challenge of developing Cambridgeshire's countryside for the future has the following objectives:

1. Increase people's awareness of landscape quality.

2. Mobilise care and action amongst the main bodies who play the most active role in generating tomorrow's landscapes.

3. Improve overall visual quality and strengthen the contrasts between landscapes in different parts of the County (emphasising a sense of place).

4. Integrate wildlife conservation into landscape action at all scales from planning at a county level, through site planning, design and management, to the detailing of 'hard' and 'soft' features at the smallest scale.

5. Protect and enhance historic features.

6. Conserve existing features and create landmarks and 'personality' in the landscape.

COUNTRYSIDE CHANGE BY DESIGN

Whilst high landscape quality is related to habitat quality, it is strongly influenced by visual characteristics. In this sense, our perception of high quality countryside landscapes is little different in principle to our perception of high quality buildings or townscape.

We readily accept that high quality architecture, urban compositions or parks are the product of a conscious, creative design process. Traditionally, however, design has rarely been associated with the rural landscape, except in relation to better examples of afforestation and (occasionally) in terms of designing large structures to 'blend in' with their surroundings.

The reason for this is that most of the countryside has, in a sense, been thought of as 'looking after itself'. Woodlands, hedgerows, stone walls, villages, ancient landmarks and other features have contrived, in their apparent (but not real) timelessness to give us landscapes of considerable quality and character without the need for professional landscape and other design inputs. Today, with evidence that the process of change often degrades rather than improves the landscape, the time has come for a fresh look at how we can reverse this trend.

Hence, these landscape guidelines are design-based; they also incorporate the potential for integrating wildlife conservation measures into the process of change. They endeavour to give practical solutions of relevance to individual projects, and emphasise the need to conceive of these in the context of the wider landscape. They offer models which can be applied in many situations throughout the County and adapted to reflect local landscape characteristics.

A CHALLENGE: SETTING NEW STANDARDS

Individual sections of this manual are aimed at developers, highway engineers, drainage engineers and farmers. Responsibility is also placed on planners to encourage higher standards, using persuasion, planning conditions or enforcement as necessary. The same principles apply to the general public, conservation volunteers and others who play a part in making the landscape.

Each section illustrates how the primary activities of these agencies impact upon the wider environment and are responsible for shaping the countryside. It is a short step, therefore, for these groups to think more positively about their roles in restoring and creating new landscapes in the decades ahead. It is necessary to think long term, to the next generation and beyond.

If Cambridgeshire's countryside is to be regenerated as proposed, it is essential for:

– developers to build care of the local landscape and sympathy for its qualities into their projects;

– farmers to remember that landscape management is part of their role as custodians of the countryside;

– road engineers to enhance the stretch of countryside through which the highway passes;

– drainage engineers to find ways of matching landscape needs with hydrological efficiency;

– local authorities to balance economy in land management with public expectations for a better environment;

– planners to ensure that all schemes which require it receive proper landscape design, provision and maintenance;

– local councils, schools and individuals to be 'landscape conscious', and to take part in practical action, wherever possible.

Near Oakington: the need for a planned approach to landscape design.

FIVE ACTION POINTS

In order to achieve the vision set out in these guidelines, the following steps will usually be necessary when considering individual projects:

1. Seek professional landscape design or management advice at the earliest possible stage in a project and before other design decisions are taken, thus ensuring an integrated design approach.

2. Understand an area's history through the study of documents, old maps, archaeological sites and ancient features; former patterns and features revealed by aerial photography can give 'clues' for the design of new features.

3. Carry out an appraisal of the local landscape to include a survey and analysis of elements such as landform, ridgelines, views, existing vegetation, wildlife habitats, soils, historical or archaeological features, built forms, local architectural styles and materials, rights of way and planning designations.

4. Ensure that the standards and design ideas set out in these guidelines, including the positive management of trees throughout their lifespan, are costed and integrated into a project at an early stage. Improved landscape standards should not be an unexpected or unwelcome financial burden but an inherent part of any project which has an impact on its surroundings.

5. Regard the costs associated with the standards set out in these guidelines as an essential part of and an investment in a project, which can add long-term value to a farm or other property, improve an owner's quality of life, and benefit the county's tourist industry; investing in a better landscape can bring economic gains.

3

FOLLOW
THE
GUIDELINES

PLANNING AND DEVELOPMENT

NEW SETTLEMENTS AND MAJOR TOWN EXPANSIONS

Proposed new settlements and major expansions of urban areas are likely during the 1990s in Cambridgeshire. Developers face the challenge of satisfying more environmentally aware purchasers, increased expectations from the public and media, and tougher planning requirements from the planning authorities. They will need to respond with positive and creative proposals which 'put something back' into the landscape.

Landscape criteria for new developments include:

– minimising impact on existing landscape qualities and features including habitats of value;

– contributing positively to landscape quality, the potential for enjoying the countryside, creative nature conservation and environmental education opportunities;

– ensuring new landscapes are endowed with sufficient management resources for securing long-term care.

Landscape design criteria should form a key aspect in the layout, form and urban

The edge of a new development, successfully linked to existing trees and hedges, at Bar Hill, near Cambridge.

design qualities of new developments. In many situations, landscape criteria may well dictate the main form of a development proposal. Whilst every situation is unique, it is expected that developers, together with their professional advisers, should:

– consider important existing views from roads, paths and public areas towards features such as church spires, fine buildings or wider landscapes, including off-site views where these may be affected by the development; avoid spoiling fine views; and consider framing or creating new views;

– pay special attention to the edges of new developments, especially where adjoining the countryside; avoid a clutter of back-garden fences, bland or repetitive building compositions and stark large-scale building masses; endeavour to achieve well-designed compositions of buildings/walls/landmarks/planting, etc. on the edges of development, including the provision of effective hedge and woodland screens;

– reflect local landscape character, particularly in the treatment of edges of developments, through the choice of appropriate native species, the pattern of woodlands/copses/hedgerows, the use of the landform and avoidance of harsh lines and the use of local materials for walls and buildings;

– seek opportunties for creative habitat enrichment e.g. through the use of open watercourses for surface water drainage in place of underground pipes and dense native species hedgerows with trees rather than ornamental shrubs or coniferous hedging.

The environmental proposals will need to be secured as part of the development through appropriate planning conditions, design briefs, masterplans and legal agreements with the local planning authorities.

The following plans or 'models' illustrate examples of how major residential and industrial developments can relate to the surrounding countryside. The models are clearly not, however, representative of all possibilities, and developers should recognise and respond to the uniqueness of each individual situation.

Residential

Edges to new residential developments can be treated positively in landscape terms.

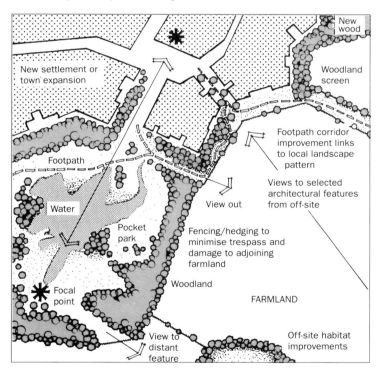

– visually diverse and attractive edges;
– habitat gain;
– countryside recreation opportunities;
– links with the wider landscape;
– farmland protected from 'urban blight'.

Industrial

When designing new industrial buildings, consider siting, massing, form and colour and the impact this will have on the wider landscape. If this is achieved satisfactorily then planting and other landscape works will enhance a good scheme. However, the only approach may be screening with dense, well-designed woodland.

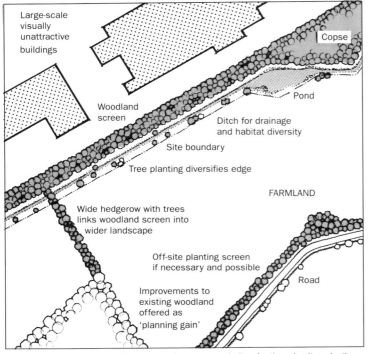

Large-scale visually unattractive buildings

Copse

Woodland screen

Pond

Ditch for drainage and habitat diversity

Site boundary

Tree planting diversifies edge

FARMLAND

Wide hedgerow with trees links woodland screen into wider landscape

Off-site planting screen if necessary and possible

Road

Improvements to existing woodland offered as 'planning gain'

– recognise that landscape features require space and allow for them in site selection and design – note landscape edge treatment is within site boundary;
– woodland screens or softens harsh industrial forms;
– seek opportunities for habitat creation;
– links with the wider landscape.

SMALL TOWNS AND VILLAGES

Development on the edges of smaller towns and villages should follow the principles set out for major developments.

Consideration of the impact of the development on the wider landscape is as important as the impact on the development site itself. Pay special attention to the design of edges, especially where they form the outer perimeter of a town or village; sometimes complete screening by means of a broad hedgerow with trees or a wider woodland belt will be an appropriate solution, but where an especially fine architectural solution can be offered, it may be appropriate to avoid screening and use planting as a foil or frame for walls, houses and other built forms.

Developers should offer appropriate on-site or off-site 'gains':

– enhance approach roads by avenue planting, for example, or use hedges as a means of screening unattractive village or town margins;
– seek opportunities for habitat creation, especially along edges to the development, e.g. in the form of hedges, copses, ditches, and ponds.

OTHER DEVELOPMENT IN THE OPEN COUNTRYSIDE

Despite the general aim of planning policy to restrict new development in the countryside, the requirements of agriculture, mineral working and waste disposal, and the demand for golf courses, etc. must be met.

Since each project is likely to present a different landscape challenge, it is not possible to offer specific guidelines which meet every case. However, the guidelines set out for housing, industry, roads, etc. may be used selectively and the guidance about landscape character in Chapter 4 will certainly apply.

Remember that new development in the countryside, although potentially damaging (especially in its early stages), can often yield positive benefits. There may

Creating attractive village edges – the sensitive integration of new development.

Harsh, poorly integrated new development.

New development integrated by means of copse, hedgerows, trees and selected views of houses.

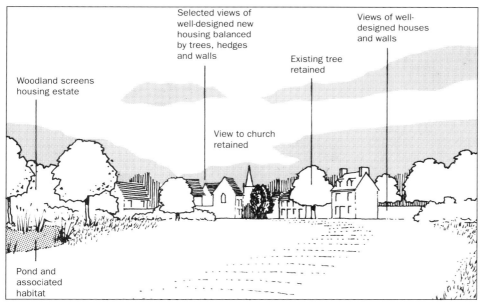

A well-designed margin between the countryside and towns and villages, combining the screening effect of woodlands and hedgerows with good architectural design and habitat gain.

New housing poorly integrated on the perimeter, Leverington, near Wisbech.

be opportunities to create a virtually new landscape or special features. Mineral workings and landfill, for example, involve a lot of earth moving which may offer possibilities for creative design.

CHECKLIST

Developers should:

– seek professional landscape and, where appropriate, ecological or archaeological advice at an early stage when considering new proposals; it is important to consider landscape, ecological and archaeological criteria at the site selection stage;

– conserve existing special features of landscape or nature conservation value;

– create new landscape features and wildlife habitats either on- or off-site, including earthworks, tree and shrub planting, woodlands, wetlands and grassland;

– ensure major developments offer environmentally based features as an integral part of the scheme. Possibilities include: woodlands, 'pocket parks', country parks, off-site landscape improvements, nature reserves, environmental teaching areas close to schools, land for informal and formal recreation and links to the countryside via existing rights of way or newly created footpaths;

– prepare management plans for landscape areas indicating requirements such as thinning regimes, intended long-term species composition and structure for new woodland areas, wetland habitat management and methods for diversifying habitats and encouraging wildlife.

Improving the approaches to existing towns and villages.

Above: a bleak approach road and harsh edge to new development detracts from the approach to village.

Below: planting along the approach road conveys a sense of arrival and retains views to significant village landmarks.

HIGHWAYS

Cambridgeshire is criss-crossed by highways, varying in scale and impact from motorways to narrow country lanes. Roads can be either major visual intrusions, sources of pollution and destroyers of landscape quality, or they can be attractive routes which take us through the countryside. Roadside trees, hedges and verges add to the richness, diversity and special character of the landscape.

Whether roads are primarily intrusions into or a means of enjoying and diversifying the countryside depends very much on scale – major roads with heavy traffic are clearly more difficult to integrate environmentally than a quiet country lane. However, design and siting are also important.

NEW ROADS AND IMPROVEMENT SCHEMES

The landscape designer can help select road alignments which minimize impact on both the immediate road corridor and the wider landscape through which the road runs. Later detailed work involves advising on the specific route and designing the associated planting, landforms and other elements.

There are likely to be major road programmes in Cambridgeshire in the years ahead. Inevitably, should projects proceed, there will be a need to minimise environmental impact. In addition, there is a need to be creative and to take advantage of the opportunities which new road construction presents. Landscape designers and engineers will be able to work together far more effectively if the road is viewed as a corridor of integrated features (road, bridges, landforms, wildlife habitats, spatial character, trees, hedges, views etc.).

ENGINEERS
Collaborate with the landscape designer at an early stage of the project and endeavour to use the road building process creatively to achieve high quality new landscapes in the countryside.

MAINTENANCE OF ROAD VERGES

Road verges probably constitute the largest area of grassland in the County. Their significance as landscape features and havens for wildlife is heightened by their prominence.

Every so often there is a surprising splash of colour, marking the few remnants of species-rich grassland which were once quite common. Around 80 such road verge sites in Cambridgeshire have now been identified and marked for protection. There are many others of more local interest.

Highway verges, which are certainly the road traveller's closest impression of the County, deserve higher standards of management. Some are illegally ploughed or excessively trimmed where this is not required for safety reasons, and others receive no cut at all.

Road verges are important as part of the highway, as landscape features and as wildlife corridors. They must not be neglected or treated as waste areas.

CHECKLIST
New Roads and Improvement Schemes

Highways engineers should:

– commission a landscape appraisal of a broad landscape corridor before routes begin to be fixed from an engineering viewpoint. Such an appraisal would not only identify aspects of the landscape which could be damaged by road construction, but would identify local landscape characteristics and seek opportunities for landscape development and management which could arise out of the road project;

– work closely with landscape architects, ecologists and archaeologists through

Principles for roads in the landscape.

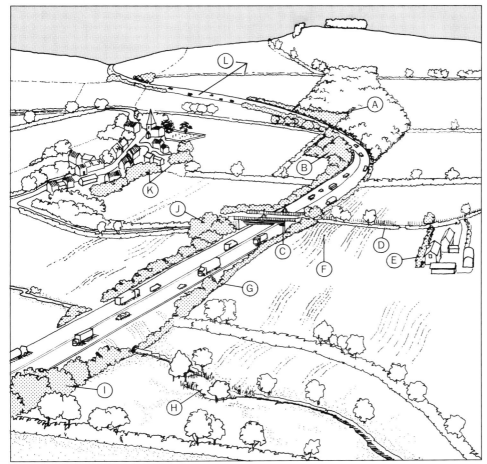

Based on *Trunk Roads: England into the 1990s,* published by the Department of Transport (1990)

A Woodland extended to roadside by planting on severed land.

B Infill planting on severed land to screen village and create new copse.

C Detailed design of bridge reflects local traditions, character and materials.

D Design of walls, fences, hedges and tree planting, etc. along side roads reflects local character.

E Off-site planting to protect farm.

F Side slopes graded out and returned to agriculture.

G New hedgerow on highway boundary.

H Alignment of road protects ponds and trees.

I Dense planting to break up scale of embankment.

J Dense planting to screen views from village.

K Off-site planting to protect village.

L Views from road to hilltop landmark help establish a 'sense of place'.

Creative opportunities on major new roads – example.

Before: New village bypass exposes views to existing housing.

After: New hedge and tree planting on verge and near housing creates interest and provides screening.

Creative opportunities on existing country roads and lanes – example.

Before

After: Verge widened and differentially mown for wildflower establishment; mixed hedge and avenue trees planted; small damp meadow and pond created; all in association with adjoining landowner.

the design process in developing a preferred route for a new road or a widening of an existing one; be prepared to place a high value on environmental factors, even if it proves difficult or impossible to price them in purely financial terms;

– where appropriate, look for ways of widening the 'road corridor' to ensure proper integration of landforms, woodlands, hedges, ponds and other features of landscape value, including wildlife habitats; look for opportunities to create significant new features adjoining the road, even if they are not required primarily to reduce the impact on the environment;

– look for opportunities, in partnership with other landowners or authorities, to improve the landscape of the wider 'zone of impact' visible from or associated with the road, thus improving the view from the road and using the process of road building to 'put something back' into the landscape;

– ensure that the design of structures and use of materials are sensitive to local land forms and establish a 'sense of place';

– establish landscape budgets where necessary for the upgrading of existing roads, as well as ensuring adequate financial provision for landscape work related to new roads.

Maintenance of Road Verges

Highway engineers and landowners should:

– maintain road verge grassland by cutting once a year (exceptions are safety zones which may require more frequent cuts and protected conservation verges which need special treatment);

– prevent illegal ploughing;

– maintain the offensive against litter;

– avoid dumping on verges and seek advice on proper restoration of disturbed grassland;

– protect and manage roadside trees and hedges and encourage new planting consistent with road safety – especially on approach roads to towns and villages.

RIVERS AND DRAINAGE

The County is roughly divided by water-courses into a north-east/south-west pattern. The lowland rivers of the Nene, Great Ouse and Cam flow towards the Wash and North Sea and in the fens have been engineered into straight channels, for drainage purposes.

The character and landscape quality of the various rivers, streams and drainage channels in the County change according to their drainage significance. The main rivers and their tributaries are characteristically sluggish with high levels of silt, their waters chemically enriched with nitrates and phosphates. Drainage engineers have been active with these rivers, working to alleviate possible flooding problems and improving field drainage. This usually implies an increase in the channel capacity and the removal of obstacles, such as projecting bushes and trees, islands and lush vegetation growth.

In the fens, the maintenance of embanked dykes and field drainage is particularly vital. Much of the land is at or below sea level and water in the dykes is often carried at a higher level with much

Before: Rivers as functional conveyors of water: flood protection measures determine landscape character; former rich lowland landscape destroyed; little or no opportunity for landscape enhancement and habitat renewal.

After: Rivers as corridors: a rich landscape area with great habitat diversity follows the river valley; meadows, marginal habitats, copses and trees create character; outside this special area, an intensive farming landscape may exist.

reliance upon pumping. The intensity of maintenance depends upon the flood risk or hazard to the surrounding land. Thus the majority of the flood banks are intensively managed by close mowing or grazing, and the channels kept clear of vegetation.

The need to secure flood alleviation has therefore destroyed many of the features which contribute to a richness of landscape character and habitat diversity. In the fens, an obviously man-made landscape, the demands of efficient drainage are necessarily overriding. However, despite this, some recent schemes have created attractive landscape features and there is great scope for landscape enrichment.

Conservation is now very much part of the remit of the National Rivers Authority (NRA) and of the drainage authorities under a code of practice 'Conservation Guidelines for Drainage Authorities'. The Water Act 1989 reinforces the earlier guidelines with a special code of practice for the NRA.

River and drainage corridors present great opportunities for improving the landscape. These should now be seized by viewing the watercourse in its wider landscape setting and integrating features such as bridges, landforms, habitats and views.

Anglian Water plc, the National Rivers Authority, the Association of Drainage Authorities, the Internal Drainage Boards and consultant drainage engineers are encouraged to:
– think creatively about the potential they have as engineers to play a part in positive landscape improvement;
– overcome procedural difficulties which may currently stand in the way of adopting the proposed broader outlook;

DRAINAGE ENGINEERS *Creative watercourse and catchment management can be used to achieve major landscape improvements; work with landscape architects to achieve new standards in the future.*

– establish management plans with effective timescales and budgets for the upgrading of existing watercourses and landholdings, as well as ensuring that there is adequate funding for landscape work associated with new drainage proposals.

CHECKLIST
Drainage engineers should:
– commission an environmental appraisal of the catchment, river valley or dyke corridor before designing any alterations. This appraisal would identify the elements of the landscape which are important in relation to the river, what could be damaged by change, and where opportunities exist for enhancement;
– work closely with landscape architects, ecologists and archaeologists through the design or management process to develop a scheme which is sympathetic to the character and quality of the watercourse whilst achieving the necessary engineering requirements;
– look to creating significant new features as well as conserving those existing features of landscape or nature conservation value. These could include areas of wetland habitats, native tree and shrub planting, willows for pollarding, and aquatic and marginal planting;
– look for opportunities, in partnership with other landowners or authorities, to improve the landscape visible from or associated with the river or dyke;
– apply the same criteria to other landholdings owned by water companies or authorities and, if appropriate, to reservoirs and larger catchments.

FARMLAND

Farmers are now thinking about their wider creative and guardianship role in the countryside. Some relish the opportunity to improve the character and diversity of the Cambridgeshire countryside. Others appreciate that landscape improvements can add to the capital value of their farm holding. This can be done more effectively if several adjoining landowners work to improve a whole tract of countryside.

THE FARM CONSERVATION PLAN

The best way to integrate landscape improvements with the efficient running of the farming operation is through a farm conservation plan.

Such a plan will ensure that wildlife conservation, rights of way management, buildings, water features, etc. are taken into account. Professional advice may be needed and grant aid is available from several sources (see pp. 83-6).

SOME IDEAS FOR FARMLAND LANDSCAPES

The following sequence of plans, representing a typical area of farmland, has been prepared as a series of models to illustrate how landscape improvements can be directed in different ways. In practice, features from some or all of the models would probably be used in designing a farm landscape plan, the balance depending on practical opportunities, the local landscape character and the character zones within the County.

TO PLANT OR NOT TO PLANT

Landscape improvement of a farm should not rely only on planting. Consider the following, for example:

1. Natural regeneration: abandoned grassland will eventually colonize with shrubs and trees to become a woodland. Natural regeneration can be an important method for creating new woodlands, with the slower initial establishment time being offset by minimal cost, natural tree forms and the typically vigorous growth of trees established from seed. The open ground and scrub stages can be as important as the final woodland for wildlife. Some management in the form of thinning and coppicing may be beneficial to give structural diversity.

2. Management of existing woodlands: seek expert advice for ancient semi-natural woodlands in particular; for other woodlands, if they are even-aged, try to create a new generation of trees through selective felling, restocking and other necessary work; plant shrubs such as hazel or holly (if appropriate to soil type and local landscape character) as well as trees; manage for long-term health and diversity of woodland types, taking into account soil type, age, and management history.

3. Open ground: open meadows, rough grassland, marshy areas, water, reed beds and other open habitats contribute in an important way to the texture of the landscape and the diversity of its habitats. In the case of chalk downlands, for example, an open landscape of grassland, with limited but carefully located tree planting, might form the primary objective.

4. Hedgerow management: avoid severe trimming of some hedgerows; allow some to grow freely; trim or

Farmland Model A1: Existing arable landscape.

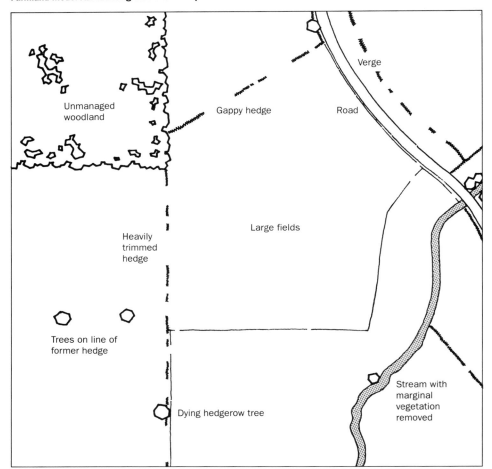

This represents 'the starting point', that is, a typical contemporary farmed landscape in Cambridgeshire.

Modern agricultural practice has removed many hedges and trees. Meadows have been ploughed.

The few remaining hedgerows are heavily trimmed and gappy; hedgerow trees are dying.

Trees and marginal vegetation have been lost along the stream through intensive cultivation and clearance. Ponds have been filled.

The woodland and occasional hedges are a reminder of the former landscape character. Declining management threatens even their continuity.

Farmland Model A2: Reinstatement of former pattern.

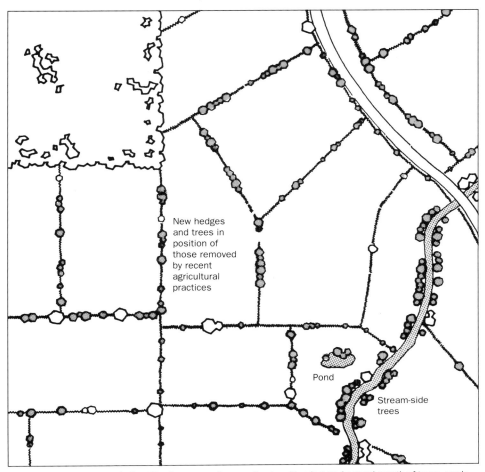

New hedges and trees in position of those removed by recent agricultural practices

Pond

Stream-side trees

Restoration of the older agricultural landscape may be possible in some areas, but it rarely suits modern agricultural methods.

Replanting hedge-lines and trees to return to former field pattern and landscape character.

Ponds, with reinstated natural growth of trees, scrub and marshy land along stream.

A small-scale landscape character.

Farmland Model A3: Planting at field corners – spinneys and copses.

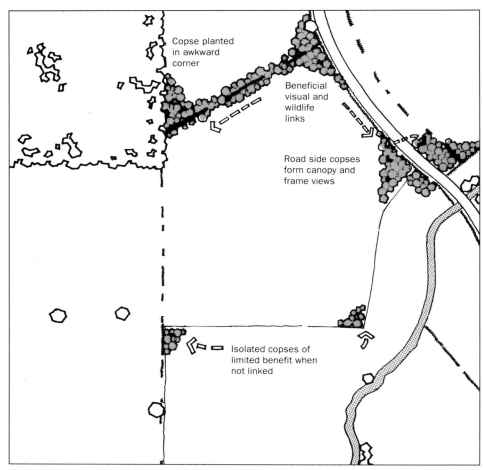

Copse planted in awkward corner

Beneficial visual and wildlife links

Road side copses form canopy and frame views

Isolated copses of limited benefit when not linked

Copse planting is a possibility in field corners which could be difficult to cultivate with large machines.

Improved tree cover with little loss of productive land.

Care is needed to ensure small isolated copses do not lead to a 'spotty' landscape character.

Linkage of copses by substantial hedgerows gives visual and ecological benefits.

Grouping copses together makes a bigger impact.

Copses on either side of a road create character and frame views.

Farmland Model A4a: Widened field margins – meadow.

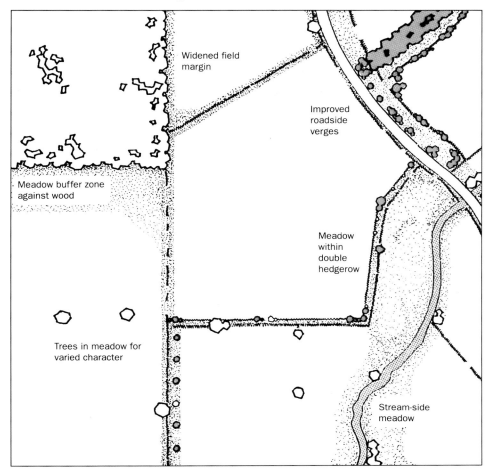

Widened field margin

Improved roadside verges

Meadow buffer zone against wood

Meadow within double hedgerow

Trees in meadow for varied character

Stream-side meadow

Zones of meadow can be created, linked to woods, hedges and streams for ecological and visual richness.

Meadows can vary in size from narrow margins to large expanses.

Linkage is important.

Meadows should relate to other habitats such as streams, woods and hedgerows.

A variety of management regimes will promote a range of wildflowers and grasses.

Farmland Model A4b: Widened field margins – woodland belts.

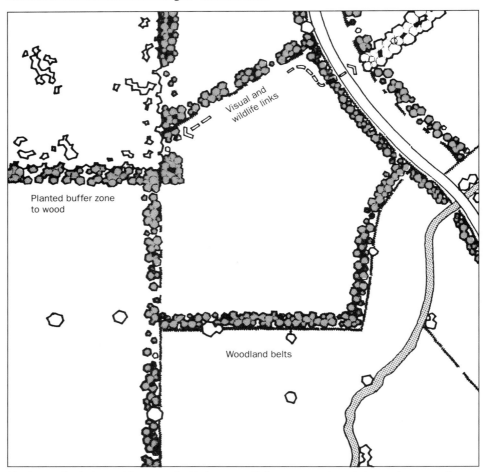

Planted buffer zone to wood

Visual and wildlife links

Woodland belts

Planting woodland edges and linear woodland belts along hedge-lines is another option.

Shrub and tree planting in widened field margins creates woodland belts.

Reinforcement of dominant hedgerows creates a new larger-scale landscape structure.

Buffer zone around an existing wood creates a diverse woodland edge.

Large-scale spaces, bold landscape structure, strong sense of enclosure.

Farmland Model A5: New woodland.

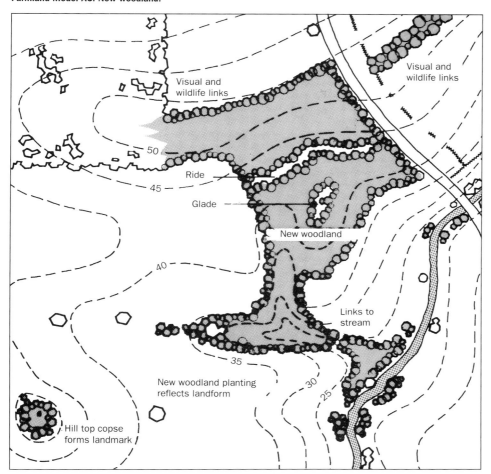

Visual and wildlife links

Visual and wildlife links

Ride

Glade

New woodland

Links to stream

New woodland planting reflects landform

Hill top copse forms landmark

New woodlands can be created with a balanced range of native species.

Planting of new woodland on land taken out of agricultural production.

Linked with existing wood for visual and wildlife benefits.

Shrubby edge to margins of wood and rides to increase species diversity and interest.

On rolling landforms, woodlands can be designed to complement the existing landform, or follow hedgerow pattern, or a combination of both (as shown here).

Farmland Model A6: Improvements to stream side and margins.

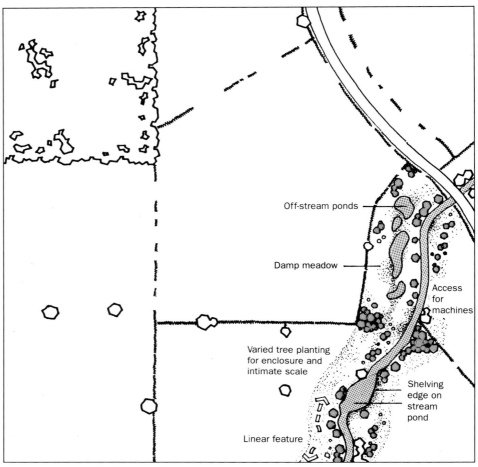

Off-stream ponds

Damp meadow

Access for machines

Varied tree planting for enclosure and intimate scale

Shelving edge on stream pond

Linear feature

Linear areas with a small-scale character and ecological diversity can be developed.

Creation of on- and off-stream ponds.

Shelving, marshy margins for habitat diversity.

Marginal and aquatic planting.

Stream-side meadows combine with complex tree pattern.

Farmland Model A7: Footpath corridor improvements.

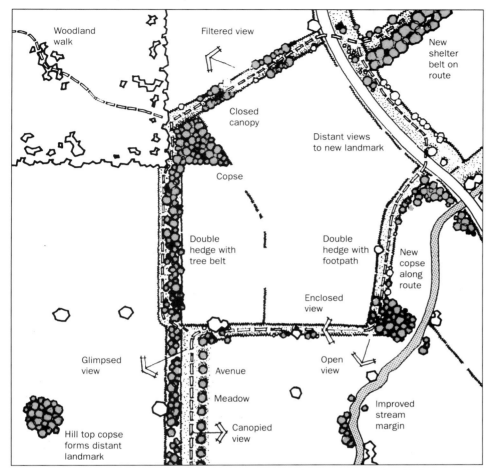

Woodland walk

Filtered view

New shelter belt on route

Closed canopy

Distant views to new landmark

Copse

Double hedge with tree belt

Double hedge with footpath

New copse along route

Enclosed view

Glimpsed view

Avenue

Open view

Meadow

Improved stream margin

Hill top copse forms distant landmark

Canopied view

Concentrate landscape improvements on linear corridors for walking and riding, by the creation of green lanes (grassy tracks, the character of which is enhanced through enclosure by hedges and/or trees along their boundaries), linked across ownership boundaries.

Footpath routes could be designed to take advantage of landscape qualities and the opportunities they present.

A variety of routes, open or enclosed by hedges, adds to the interest.

Attractive views can be enhanced by framing with planting.

A sense of scale can be conveyed, e.g. contrast a narrow route with a view across open fields.

Footpath corridor improvements: cross-sections.

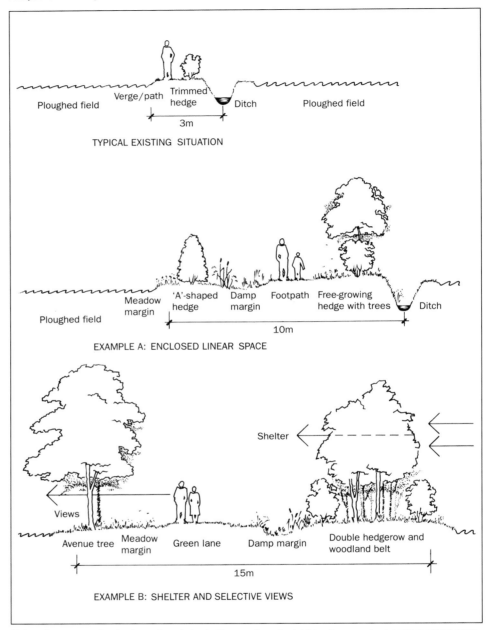

Ploughed field   Verge/path   Trimmed hedge   Ditch   Ploughed field

3m

TYPICAL EXISTING SITUATION

Ploughed field   Meadow margin   'A'-shaped hedge   Damp margin   Footpath   Free-growing hedge with trees   Ditch

10m

EXAMPLE A: ENCLOSED LINEAR SPACE

Shelter

Views

Avenue tree   Meadow margin   Green lane   Damp margin   Double hedgerow and woodland belt

15m

EXAMPLE B: SHELTER AND SELECTIVE VIEWS

Rights of way across farmland are often obstructed by ploughed ground, narrow walking surfaces, poorly maintained or absent stiles and lack of signposting.

Farmers and landowners can help by managing their land to allow access for walking along rights of way; guidance is available from the local authorities.

Important rights of way can be transformed into green lanes by the creation of landscape corridors.

coppice some sections of a hedge in rotation; allow individual tree or shrub species to grow up in a trimmed hedge; concentrate improvements and conservation on hedges which have visual significance in the wider landscape and/or are older or species rich; trim during the winter months to minimise the impact on nesting birds and food sources.

5. Water features: if there are streams or ponds on the farm, leave a margin uncultivated and develop them, with planting as necessary, to form a visually and ecologically valuable feature; even a 5m wide margin can be of value, but the wider the better. Although you are dependent to some extent on the actions of neighbouring landowners there is much you can do to maintain water quality in your streams and ponds through sound management.

6. Archaeological sites: particular care should be taken to avoid damage to moated sites and to all traces of medieval earthworks. They should be kept clear of trees and scrub. Cleaning of moats is encouraged, provided archaeological advice is followed. Landscape work near village edges also needs care, as these small villages have often shrunk or shifted, leaving medieval earthworks in pasture fields.

CHECKLIST

Farmers and landowners should:
  – consider their roles as custodians and managers of the rural landscape as well as producers of agricultural products in a business context;
  – place a high priority on avoiding

environmental damage including damage to archaeological sites through agricultural practices;
  – look for opportunities to make a positive contribution to landscape quality, including habitat creation and management;
  – be aware of the importance of conserving special features in the landscape, such as species-rich hedges that may form ancient parish or other boundaries, ancient semi-natural woodlands, visually important 'landmarks' such as hill-top tree groups or road-side avenues, ponds, marshy areas, moats, burial mounds and other historic monuments, all of which contribute to the richness and diversity of the countryside and which may have a story to tell in an historical sense;
  – pay attention to small-scale details such as bridges over ditches, stone walls, individually crafted gates, farm signs and gnarled old trees, which all add to the quality of landscape; these should be carefully conserved and they should provide the creative inspiration for new features in the countryside;
  – consider the visual impact of farm buildings and structures and look for ways of integrating them in the landscape; soften the impact of new structures by careful consideration of location, design, colour and associated planting;
  – use native species appropriate to the locality (see planting guidelines in Chapter 4); if possible use plants of local provenance (e.g. grown from seed from old trees on the farm) or where this is not possible, at least assure British origin (an oak from Germany,

for example, whilst it may be of the same species as our English Oak, may be genetically different);
– prepare a farm conservation plan which will integrate landscape improvements, wildlife and archaeological conservation, and rights of way management with the efficient running of the farming operation;
– prepare such a plan in co-operation with adjoining farmers and landowners so that each landholding is integrated in a wider context and contributes to the landscape character of the area as a whole;
– set aside a 'landscape budget' each year for environmental improvement, as even a small investment will, over the years, make an impact; ensure even minor works are carried out in the context of an overall masterplan or long-term strategy – a small amount of well-placed planting is better than a larger amount scattered throughout the farm;
– remember that valuable grants, professional advice and even volunteer helpers are available to put the landscape plan into action;
– think long-term; the character of today's finest landscapes can often be traced to planting or management regimes going back one or two centuries or more – similarly, today's generation needs to plan for the decades and centuries ahead.

4

CHERISH LANDSCAPE CHARACTER

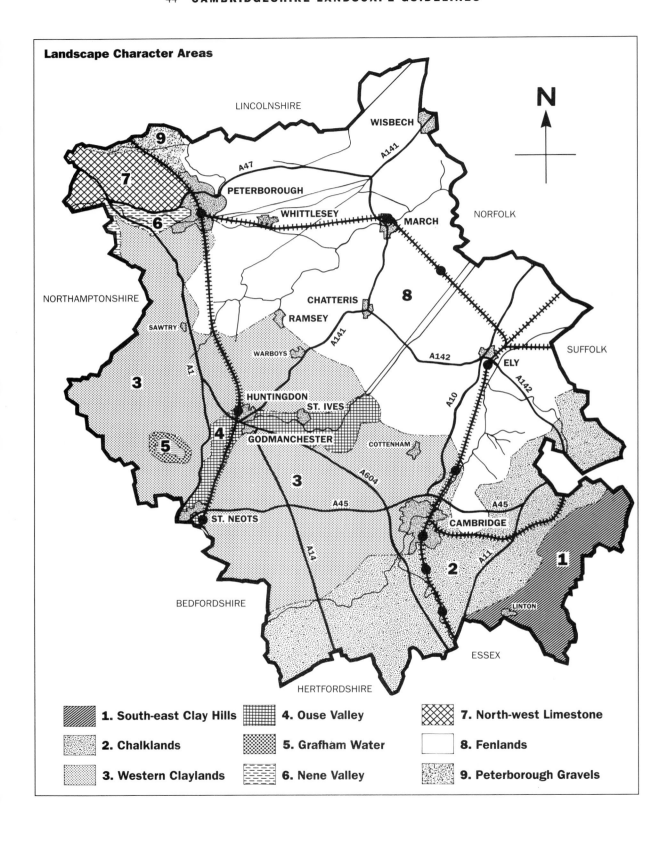

Landscape Character Areas

1. South-east Clay Hills	4. Ouse Valley	7. North-west Limestone
2. Chalklands	5. Grafham Water	8. Fenlands
3. Western Claylands	6. Nene Valley	9. Peterborough Gravels

One of the central objectives of these guidelines is that design and management in the countryside should be more responsive to place: that is, different landscapes should be sustained in different parts of the County, reflecting the underlying geology, landform and history of land management.

For this purpose the County has been divided into character areas on the basis of distinctive existing landscape characters.

When planning new landscape works you are asked to respond to and build upon the key features of the existing landscape and also to create new features in a co-ordinated and planned landscape renewal programme.

The recommended plant species given for each character area have a sound basis, but local variations do exist and each design should be responsive to the conditions and opportunities of each individual site.

The map illustrates the locations of the character areas.

AREA 1: SOUTH-EAST CLAY HILLS

This is an undulating area, quite high for Cambridgeshire, at about 100–120m above sea level on the hilltops. The small villages and hamlets have developed in more sheltered situations, usually along the springline in the shallow valleys.

Dense woodland and heavy soils deterred prehistoric farmers. By medieval times all our present villages had been founded, although these are often recognisably later and less successful than villages to the east or west. Moated sites are common, making use of water-retentive soil to give protection to homesteads in a newly settled landscape.

Landscape character derives from the scattering of farmsteads, and small settlements interspersed with farm woodlands. The field sizes are large, but are united by the gently rolling landform and woodlands. Earth banks are a distinctive feature along some roadsides, appearing to be a relic from the historic hedge and bank field boundaries; a few still retain their hedges. Elsewhere surviving hedges, often without trees, are trimmed low and can create a mean appearance to the landscape.

PRINCIPLES FOR LANDSCAPE IMPROVEMENT AND MANAGEMENT IN THE SOUTH-EAST CLAY HILLS

Generally this is a small-scale and satisfactorily composed landscape with enclosure and form provided by the gently rolling landform and woodland blocks. Nevertheless, improvements could usefully be directed towards the following principles:

1. Management of existing woodlands: ancient semi-natural woodlands are important landscape, historical and nature conservation features, and those in the area should be carefully conserved. Enhancement of other woodlands could include selective felling and re-stocking, while most woods would benefit from the creation of 'edge areas' (see Farmland Models A4a and A4b on pp. 35–6).

2. Creation of new woodlands: ideally these should extend or link with existing woods, but free-standing

South-east clay hills:
Carlton.

woods of 2–5 hectares or more in the area would have a significant impact (see Farmland Model A5 on p. 37). They should be carefully sited with regard to:
– existing or potential views;
– wildlife potential;
– landform and skyline;
– the broader pattern of the landscape.

3. Planting woodland belts and widened hedgerows: this will create bold linear elements which link woods and copses; if sensitively placed for maximum impact, such belts need not involve large areas of land (see Farmland Model A4b on p. 36).

4. Hedgerow management: simple enhancement of the landscape could be achieved by allowing selected existing hedges to grow taller; those hedges with the strongest visual and wildlife potential should be selected for this purpose. Historically significant hedgerows should be carefully conserved.

5. Village edges: where unsightly fringes to villages meet farmland, woodland belts or broad hedgerows can be used for screening where land is available. Views from roads can be

SOUTH-EAST CLAY HILLS Before: A rural landscape with great opportunities for improvement.

Undulating landform gives shelter to small village.

Large open fields subdivided by low hedges.

Small woodlands on skyline.

SOUTH-EAST CLAY HILLS After: A richer landscape with woods, taller hedgerows, meadow margins, stream landscape corridor and improved village edge.

Additional planting improves village setting.

Hedgerows allowed to grow taller to give small-scale enclosure.

Enlarged woodlands give broad-scale enclosure.

obscured by planting along the road margin. It is important to retain or frame particularly important views of distant skylines, fine village views, church towers, etc. and in these situations, a more open village edge, possibly with short avenues on the entrance roads, will be more appropriate.

6. Footpath corridor improvements: landscape enhancement to local footpaths is needed along selected routes (see Farmland Model A7 on p. 39).

PLANT SPECIES GUIDELINES FOR THE SOUTH-EAST CLAY HILLS
Clay soils (except valley bottoms and wet sites)

Mixed Woodlands
Quercus robur (oak)
  dominant tree, mixed woodlands.
Fraxinus excelsior (ash)
  dominant tree, mixed woodlands.
Prunus avium (wild cherry)
  less common, mixed woodlands.
Acer campestre (field maple)
  glades, near edges.
Corylus avellana (hazel)
  dominant shrub, edges, glades, scrub.
Crataegus monogyna (hawthorn)
  near edges, mixed thickets.
Sambucus nigra (elder)
  occasional, understorey and edges.

Hedgerows, woodland edges and scrub
Crataegus monogyna (hawthorn)
Corylus avellana (hazel)
Prunus spinosa (blackthorn)
Rosa canina (dog rose)
Malus sylvestris (crab apple)

Acer campestre (field maple)
Cornus sanguinea (dogwood)
  occasional.

Trees in hedgerows
Quercus robur (oak)
  dominant.
Fraxinus excelsior (ash)
  sub-dominant.
Acer campestre (field maple)
  sub-dominant.

Avenues
Quercus robur (oak)
Tilia sp. (lime)
Aesculus hippocastanum (horse chestnut)
  environs of villages only.
Avenues – all as single species, not mixed.

Stream sides, wet clay soils
Alnus glutinosa (alder)
  dominant, in copses, small groups and river banks.
Salix alba (white willow)
  sub-dominant; not in mixes.
Salix fragilis (crack willow)
  forms typical pollarded trees, also river banks.
Salix caprea (goat willow)
  scrubby copses.
Corylus avellana (hazel)
  occasional on stream banks if not waterlogged.
Populus tremula (aspen)
  in thickets; not in mixes.
Fraxinus excelsior (ash)
  occasional where not waterlogged.
Quercus robur (oak)
  occasional where not waterlogged.
Viburnum opulus (guelder rose)
  occasional as individuals and small groups.
Cornus sanguinea (dogwood)
  occasional as individuals and small groups.

Chalklands: Babraham.

AREA 2: CHALKLANDS

The complex history of settlement and the impact of people on the landscape over the centuries is particularly apparent in this part of the County. Roman roads, Anglo-Saxon earthworks, large fields, modern roads and developments are all interlinked.

The region was mostly too dry for early settlement. However, this dryness and light vegetation meant that it was ideal for communications and it is traversed by a major prehistoric and historic highway, the Icknield Way. Its importance as a highway also gave it strategic value. In the Iron Age it was controlled by Wandlebury hill fort and in Anglo-Saxon times by the three great linear dykes which span the chalkland from the fen edge east of Cambridge to the wooded edge on the higher claylands (a fourth 'Bran Ditch' near Fowlmere has been almost completely destroyed).

These artificial elements overlie the smooth rolling chalkland hills. The hills are dissected by the two gentle valleys of the Granta and the Rhee, which converge to form the River Cam just south of Cambridge.

The area was used for sheep farming well into the nineteenth century, leading to the creation of botanically rich grasslands which now only survive in well-protected locations.

The majority of the chalkland is devoted to growing cereal crops, despite the frequently poor, thin soils. It is a broad-scale landscape of large fields, low

CHALKLANDS Before

A denuded, intensely arable landscape.

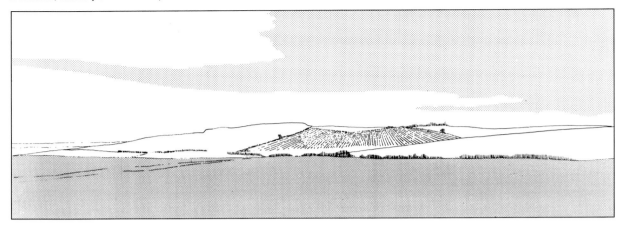

CHALKLANDS After

Smooth, rolling profile to rising ground.

Wooded escarpment emphasises landform.

Beech hanger forms strong focal point on brow of hill.

Good hedgerows and woodlands emphasise rolling landform and give sense of scale.

mechanically trimmed hedges and few trees. The eastern part of this area has a number of woodlands and shelter belts which help to break up the long distant views and give some form and character. Certain high points have small beech copses or 'hangers' which are prominent and characteristic features in the open landscape.

The essentially geometrical field pattern resulting from the downland hedge enclosure is further subdivided in an area to the south-west of Newmarket. Here the relatively modern growth and prosperity of the racehorse industry has imposed a distinctive pattern of small, tree-lined paddocks, which imparts a well-wooded character to the area. This has arisen from the need to provide shelter from cold winds and driving rain and also visual enclosure, to avoid external movements frightening the young horses. The stud farms are expanding away from the immediate surroundings of Newmarket, and no doubt their landscape pattern will also follow.

A rich and characterful river corridor; classic lowland landscapes can be recreated with the right design and management skills.

PRINCIPLES FOR LANDSCAPE IMPROVEMENT AND MANAGEMENT IN THE CHALKLANDS

The future pattern is for a large-scale landscape defined by rolling hills, large fields, bold shelter belts, sweeping masses of woodland and occasional beech hangers.

1. Planting new beech hangers: could be placed on suitable, carefully sited knolls, hilltops and scarp-tops; these would form focal points to reinforce the local chalklands landscape character.

2. Management and creation of chalk grasslands: the majority of the grasslands should remain open and uncluttered. The promotion of species-rich grassland on thin chalk soils would provide visual and wildlife value. Road verges should also be managed to promote plant diversity and interest.

3. Management of existing shelter belts: these should be restocked to encourage young tree growth and fill gaps.

4. Planting new mixed woodlands and shelter belts: carefully sited to enclose large tracts of rolling farmland and emphasise landforms (see Farmland Models A4b and A5 on pp. 36–7).

5. Creation of landscape corridors along river valleys: the valleys of the Rivers Granta, Rhee and Cam have a distinct small-scale intimacy which contrasts well with the surrounding chalklands. Small woods and wetland meadows could be supplemented with copses, lines of willows to be pollarded, and areas of marginal and aquatic vegetation (see Farmland Model A6 on p. 38).

6. Hedgerows: selected hedgerows should be reinforced, or managed for particularly significant impact, based upon their visual and wildlife potential. Historically significant hedgerows should be carefully conserved, and new hedges planted to emphasise the existing landscape.

7. Footpath corridor improvements: the Roman Road is an important route across the chalk landscape. Planting small woodlands at selected locations such as hill tops or to frame views, as well as carefully managing the existing rich flora, would enhance the route.

A similar approach could be adopted for other footpaths in the area, concentrating on a small number of linked corridors (see Farmland Model A7 on p. 39).

8. Road corridor improvements: the M11 has had minimal planting to soften its impact on the landscape. The planting of selected embankments and adjacent field margins with native trees and shrubs would provide interest for those using the road as well as helping to integrate the road with the surrounding countryside.

9. Conservation of the linear dykes: selective removal of scrub growth and re-establishment of sheep grazing, if possible, would enable the massive scale of these historic earthworks to be appreciated and promote chalk grass and flora communities. Some areas of scrub should be retained for habitat and visual diversity. The significance of the dykes in the landscape could be reinforced by managing adjacent strips of agricultural land as grassland or scrub.

10. Newmarket stud farms: new investment in the expansion of stud farms is causing significant change. Shelter belts should be planned on less rigid lines and should respond more to the local landforms, hedges, copses and roads. The shelterbelts should be planted with native tree and shrub species for visual and wildlife benefits.

PLANT SPECIES GUIDELINES FOR THE CHALKLANDS

Beech hangers

Fagus sylvatica (beech)
plus occasional additions of species from 'mixed woodlands' below.

Mixed woodlands

Fagus sylvatica (beech)
dominant mainly on shallow chalk soils where it may form large stands; smaller groups in more diverse woods.

Fraxinus excelsior (ash)
dominant; mixed woods.

Tilia cordata (small-leaved lime)
less common.

Carpinus betulus (hornbeam)
less common.

Prunus avium (wild cherry)
less common.

Taxus baccata (yew)
small groups.

Corylus avellana (hazel)
dominant shrub, understorey, edges, glades, scrub.

Acer campestre (field maple)
glades, near edges.

Crataegus monogyna (hawthorn)
near edges, mixed thickets.

Sambucus nigra (elder)
occasional, understorey and edges.

Ligustrum vulgaris (wild privet)
occasional, edges.

Viburnum lantana (wayfaring tree)
  occasional, edges.

Note: beech should be planted in single species groups of at least 500 sq. m. when used in woodland block; do not use in random mixes.

Hedgerows, woodland edges and scrub

Crataegus monogyna (hawthorn)
Corylus avellana (hazel)
Prunus spinosa (blackthorn)
Acer campestre (field maple)
Rosa canina (dog rose)
Ligustrum vulgaris (wild privet)
  occasional.
Viburnum lantana (wayfaring tree)
  occasional.

Trees in hedgerows/avenues

Fraxinus excelsior (ash)
  dominant, hedgerows.
Fagus sylvatica (beech)
  mostly avenues; some hedgerows.
Acer campestre (field maple)
  sub-dominant, hedgerows.

Avenues – all as single species, not mixed. Hedgerows – mixed.

AREA 3: WESTERN CLAYLANDS

As in the South-eastern Claylands, dense woodland and heavy soils deterred prehistoric farmers, and even Roman settlements are not commonly found in these regions. Population pressure and the use of improved ploughs, however, led to many medieval settlements which have

since been deserted or have shrunken to tiny hamlets or single farms. Ridge and furrow (a survival of medieval ploughing), deserted medieval villages, such as Wintringham, Weald and Washingley, and other substantial medieval settlement earthworks, such as those at Steeple and Little Gidding, Hamerton, and Winwick, together with numerous moated sites and ruined churches (at Denton and Woolley) are now all features of this sparsely populated landscape.

This gently undulating landscape is subdivided by the shallow Ouse Valley (landscape area 4). It consists of large-scale arable farmland with open fields, sparse trimmed hedgerows and watercourses often cleared of bankside vegetation. There are scattered woodlands and approximately half of these are ancient semi-natural woodlands of considerable importance in the County context. The biggest concentration of woodlands is in the south-west corner of the County. Elsewhere individual woods are of importance in visual and nature conservation terms, but they tend to be isolated incidents in an area dominated by arable farmland.

The landscape of this part of Cambridgeshire has been greatly affected by modern agricultural practices. Increased mechanisation has led to the removal of hedgerows and amalgamation of fields. Many of the remaining hedges are `gappy' and trimmed almost out of existence by regular cutting. Dutch Elm Disease has taken a considerable toll of hedgerow trees, and the extensive replanting which is still young has yet to make any major impact, although with over one million grant-aided trees having been planted since 1974 significant change is likely over the next

Western Claylands:
Boxworth.

few decades. Marginal land has been brought into production by drainage and other soil improvements. Larger farm units have created a need for large storage buildings, which can be prominent in the landscape.

Small villages and hamlets are scattered throughout the area, usually in sheltered places with existing trees. Small grass paddocks typically occur on the edges of the villages. Church spires and towers enliven the skyline.

Existing and former wartime airfields at Alconbury, Wyton, Molesworth, Glatton, Warboys, Upwood, Kimbolton, Graveley, Staughton, Sibson, Bourn and Great Gransden have a significant impact on the area.

PRINCIPLES FOR LANDSCAPE IMPROVEMENT AND MANAGEMENT IN THE WESTERN CLAYLANDS

It would be unrealistic and inappropriate to attempt to restore the pre-war landscape of smaller fields with tree-lined hedges. Instead a new landscape pattern that responds to the demands of both modern agricultural practice and the need for landscape enhancement is necessary. The vision is one of a fairly large-scale landscape with large rolling fields enclosed by and sweeping around blocks and belts of woodland and broad hedgerows. In the valley bottoms, the objective should be to create smaller-scaled stream-side landscape zones with trees, copses, meadows and other features.

Where remnants of the old ridge and furrow survive as grassland or in woodland they should be preserved.

Creation of the new landscape structure should be directed towards the following principles:

1. **Management of existing woodlands:** the careful management of ancient semi-natural woodlands and selective re-stocking and creation of 'edge areas' elsewhere (see Farmland Model A4b on p. 36) is essential.

2. **Creation of new woodlands:** ideally these should be at least 2 hectares in size and located so that they make a major impact in relation to:
– viewing points;
– wildlife potential;
– landform and skylines.

The new woodland blocks may be planted to reflect landforms, thus developing a new character of wooded

WESTERN CLAYLANDS **Before**

Dead tree.	Very little sense of landform or enclosure.	Poor, sparse hedgerows.	Large, modern farm buildings prominent on the skyline.	Small scrubland on land difficult to cultivate.

WESTERN CLAYLANDS **After**

Dead tree retained for hole-nesting birds. Saplings selected from hedge and allowed to grow untrimmed.	Tree line on horizon helps to tie features together and enclose the space.	Hedgerows emphasise landform and give character; tree planting in hedge.	Farm buildings well screened by planting.	Woodland on horizon provides good backdrop.	New woodland forms strong feature.

skylines, distinctive clumps and woodlands following the folds in the land. Elsewhere, woodlands may be planted to reflect the existing or former field patterns, thus being derived from the inherited pattern (see Farmland Model A5 on p. 37). In practice, a combination of these two approaches would emerge, reflecting both old and new landscape patterns.

3. Planting of woodland belts: probably based on existing hedgerows, linking woodland blocks, the belts should be carefully aligned to reinforce landforms and would enclose large areas of rolling farmland (see Farmland Model A4b on p. 36).

4. Creation of landscape corridors in valley bottoms: this will necessitate setting aside 5–15m or more either side of streams to create semi-wooded corridors of diverse habitats (see Farmland Model A6 on p. 38).

5. Hedgerows: selected hedgerows should be reinforced or managed for particularly significant impact, based upon their visual and wildlife potential. Historically significant hedgerows should be carefully conserved, and new hedges planted to emphasise the existing landscape.

6. Road margins: verges should be managed for flc al diversity; hedgerows with trees should be concentrated on lower slopes to prevent loss of views from higher land and planted to create a bold sequence of enclosed and open characters appropriate to the large scale of the landscape (see Farmland Models A4a and A4b on pp. 35–6).

7. Footpath corridor improvements: a small number of long-distance routes and also circular/linking routes related to villages and towns should be located, and landscape improvements implemented along their alignments; ideally these features will be integrated with other new features as in 1 and 4 above (see Farmland Model A7 on p. 39).

8. Village approaches: increased tree cover with trees along road margins, woodland belts alongside roads, planting at edges of villages and hedgerow planting is desirable; it is important to ensure key views are not lost.

9. Old airfields: there may be unsightly buildings which require fresh landscape treatment.

10. Urban fringe: where the claylands border the Ouse Valley towns (St Ives, Huntingdon, St Neots) a substantial increase in tree and hedge cover is needed with trees along road margins, and woodland belts alongside roads and the edges of developments.

PLANT SPECIES GUIDELINES FOR THE WESTERN CLAYLANDS
Clay soils (except valley bottoms and wet sites)

Mixed woodlands
Quercus robur (oak) dominant tree.
Fraxinus excelsior (ash) dominant tree.
Prunus avium (wild cherry) less common.
Acer campestre (field maple) glades, near edges.

Corylus avellana (hazel)
dominant shrub, edges, glades, scrub.
Crataegus monogyna (hawthorn)
near edges, mixed thickets.
Sambucus nigra (elder)
occasional, understorey and edges.

Hedgerows, woodland edges and scrub
Crataegus monogyna (hawthorn)
Corylus avellana (hazel)
Prunus spinosa (blackthorn)
Rosa canina (dog rose)
Acer campestre (field maple)
Malus sylvestris (crab apple)
Cornus sanguinea (dogwood)
occasional.

Trees in hedgerows
Quercus robur (oak)
dominant.
Fraxinus excelsior (ash)
sub-dominant.
Acer campestre (field maple)
sub-dominant.

Avenues
Quercus robur (oak)
Tilia sp. (lime)
Aesculus hippocastanum (horse chestnut)
environs of villages only.
Avenues – all as single species, not mixed.

Stream sides, wet clay soils
Alnus glutinosa (alder)
dominant, in copses and small groups.
Salix alba (white willow)
sub-dominant, not in mixes.
Salix fragilis (crack willow)
typical pollarded tree.
Salix caprea (goat willow)
scrubby copses.

Fraxinus excelsior (ash)
occasional where not waterlogged.
Quercus robur (oak)
occasional where not waterlogged.
Corylus avellana (hazel)
occasional on stream banks if not waterlogged.
Populus tremula (aspen)
in thickets; not in mixes.
Viburnum opulus (guelder rose)
occasional as individuals and small groups.
Cornus sanguinea (dogwood)
occasional as individuals and small groups.

AREA 4: OUSE VALLEY

Rivers provided a major means of communication until very recent times, and also a good water supply. Light, well-drained gravel soils were ideal for prehistoric agriculture and also attracted Roman and Anglo-Saxon farmers. Roman, medieval (and most modern) towns were situated on river crossings (e.g. Huntingdon/Godmanchester, St Ives, St Neots) and river valleys have always been the most populated areas.

The meandering River Ouse in its shallow valley bisects the claylands that form the western edge of Cambridgeshire. The margins of the river consist of a mosaic of flood plains and grazing meadows, working and disused gravel pits and lakes, sprawling housing areas and industrial estates. Elsewhere, the Ouse Valley is characterised by thick hedges, trees and fields.

Ouse Valley: St Ives.

PRINCIPLES FOR LANDSCAPE IMPROVEMENT AND MANAGEMENT IN THE OUSE VALLEY

The River Ouse, with its distinctive floodplain meadows, hedgerows and trees forms the basic landscape character of the area; but this is now much influenced by flooded gravel pits and urban expansion. In certain places the area's landscape character has declined markedly as a result of development. There is, therefore, a need to create a bold landscape framework which unifies and enhances many of these disparate uses, creating a rich and interesting river corridor with a diverse mix of open and enclosed spaces.

Under the provisions of the Cambridgeshire Aggregates (Minerals) Local Plan opportunities for further mineral working along the Ouse Valley corridor are limited. Proposals for extraction, restoration and after use will be determined with reference to both county and district local plan policies and landscape guidelines.

The new landscape envisaged can be created by following the principles below:

1. Creation of a riverside landscape corridor: allocating zones 10–30m wide (increasing where possible up to the full width of the floodplain) either side of the river would conserve and/or produce a landscape of bankside trees, such as willows and alders, together with wet grazing meadows, marshlands and areas of open water (see Farmland Model A6 on p. 38).

2. Plantations of riverside willows and poplars: these would quickly provide strong elements of enclosure or screening where necessary.

3. Planting bankside willows to be pollarded: carefully sited, these would add character and interest to parts of the river corridor.

4. Small copses and large hedgerows: a framework should be established away from the river that could accommodate a number of competing uses (see Farmland Model A4b on p. 36).

5. Creation of meadows: especially in the riverside areas and close to settlements.

6. Development edges: woodland belts along the edges of development or roads would be valuable in screening unsightly views.

PLANT SPECIES GUIDELINES FOR THE OUSE VALLEY
Clay soils (except valley bottoms and wet sites)

Mixed woodlands

Quercus robur (oak)
  dominant tree.
Fraxinus excelsior (ash)
  dominant tree.
Prunus avium (wild cherry)
  less common.
Acer campestre (field maple)
  glades, near edges.
Corylus avellana (hazel)
  dominant shrub, edges, glades, scrub.
Crataegus monogyna (hawthorn)
  near edges, mixed thickets.
Sambucus nigra (elder)
  occasional, understorey and edges.

A rich and interesting river corridor of open meadows with bankside trees, enclosed by large hedges and tree belts.

Hedgerows, woodland edges and scrub

Crataegus monogyna (hawthorn)

Corylus avellana (hazel)

Prunus spinosa (blackthorn)

Rosa canina (dog rose)

Acer campestre (field maple)

Malus sylvestris (crab apple)

Cornus sanguinea (dogwood)
  occasional.

Trees in hedgerows

Quercus robur (oak)
  dominant.

Fraxinus excelsior (ash)
  sub-dominant.

Salix alba (white willow)
  dominant.

Acer campestre (field maple)
  sub-dominant.

Avenues

Quercus robur (oak)

Tilia sp. (lime)

Aesculus hippocastanum (horse chestnut)
  environs of villages only.

Avenues - all as single species, not mixed.

Stream sides, wet clay soils

Alnus glutinosa (alder)
  dominant, in copses, small groups and
  river banks.

Salix alba (white willow)
  sub-dominant; not in mixes.

Salix fragilis (crack willow)
  forms typical pollarded trees, also river
  banks.

Salix caprea (goat willow)
  scrubby copses.

Corylus avellana (hazel)
  occasional on stream banks if not
  waterlogged.

Populus tremula (aspen)
  in thickets; not in mixes.

Viburnum opulus (guelder rose)
  occasional as individuals and small
  groups.

Cornus sanguinea (dogwood)
  occasional as individuals and small
  groups.

Fraxinus excelsior (ash)
  occasional where not waterlogged.

Quercus robur (oak)
  occasional where not waterlogged.

Gravel soils

Alnus glutinosa (alder)
  dominant, copses, small groups, river
  banks.

Populus alba (white poplar)
  occasional, individuals, small groups.

Populus canescens (grey poplar)
  occasional, individuals, small thickets.

Salix caprea (goat willow)
  scrub, thickets, not mixed.

Salix alba (white willow)
  sub-dominant, not in mixes.

Quercus robur (oak)
  occasional, drier conditions, hedgerows,
  woodlands.

Fraxinus excelsior (ash)
  occasional, drier conditions, hedgerows,
  woodlands.

AREA 5: GRAFHAM WATER

Grafham Water is an example of a major
new man-made landscape feature. The
flooding of a shallow valley to make the
third largest man-made lake in England has
provided a locally important centre for
water-based recreation and nature
conservation. However, this is one
instance where the provision of water has

not improved the landscape or scenic qualities of the area; a great opportunity has been lost.

The reservoir has an 'introverted' and secluded character. It is separated from the surrounding area by low, intensively farmed hills and small woods. In many situations a combination of hilly land and water provides a fine basis for an interesting landscape, but here the hills are too insignificant to enclose views across the lake, yet they define an easily identifiable boundary which prevents any sense of concealment or mystery about the size of the lake. Similarly the woodlands are not sufficiently well related to form a strong

visual feature in the landscape.

Even so, Grafham Water is an area which is used by a large number of people. For this reason, a programme of landscape enhancement coupled with the recreational uses would be very worthwhile.

PRINCIPLES FOR LANDSCAPE IMPROVEMENT AND MANAGEMENT IN THE GRAFHAM WATER AREA

1. Linking together existing woodland: new woodlands or strong woodland belts should be designed to form an interesting diverse margin to the reservoir. A series of spaces would be created which would be small-scale

Grafham Water: western shore.

and sheltered and would enclose views onto and from the water. Priority for this work would relate to significant improvements to existing facilities such as the watersports centre, public car parks, picnic areas and viewpoints. Landform and skyline would be emphasised by woodland planting.

2. Management of existing woodlands: integrated with 1 above, it would be important to ensure the careful management of ancient semi-natural woodlands and the long-term health of other existing woods by selective felling, re-stocking and the creation of varied edge types (see Farmland Model A4b on p. 36).

3. Creation of sheltered margins to the reservoir sides: marginal and aquatic plants could be established along the shores. This would reduce erosion of the shorelines and add variety and interest to the foreground of views across the water.

4. Arable margins: the creation of a transitional zone of meadows with copses and individual trees between the arable farmland and the shore would help to add some character. Combined with 3 above, an interesting, attractive landscape could be developed.

5. Stream corridors: a number of small streams feed into the reservoir. The creation of semi-wooded corridors along the stream sides would spread the influence of the transitional areas suggested in 4 above (see Farmland Model A6 on p. 38).

6. Footpath corridor improvements: there are a number of footpaths which link the reservoir with the surrounding small villages. These should be co-ordinated by the principles outlined above in order to provide an attractive series of recreational routes around the reservoir (see Farmland Model A7 on p. 39).

7. Public car parks and picnic areas: these areas are critical in formulating public impressions of the site. Landscape works, including planting to provide shelter, enclosure, direction of views and interest would be valuable in achieving significant improvements.

PLANT SPECIES GUIDELINES FOR THE GRAHAM WATER AREA
Clay soils (except valley bottoms and wet sites)

Mixed woodlands

Quercus robur (oak)
  dominant tree.
Fraxinus excelsior (ash)
  dominant tree.
Prunus avium (wild cherry)
  less common.
Acer campestre (field maple)
  glades, near edges.
Corylus avellana (hazel)
  dominant shrub, edges, glades, scrub.
Crataegus monogyna (hawthorn)
  near edges, mixed thickets.
Sambucus nigra (elder)
  occasional, understorey and edges.

Hedgerows, woodland edges and scrub

Crataegus monogyna (hawthorn)
Corylus avellana (hazel)
Prunus spinosa (blackthorn)
Rosa canina (dog rose)
Acer campestre (field maple)
Malus sylvestris (crab apple)
Cornus sanguinea (dogwood)
  occasional.

Trees in hedgerows

Quercus robur (oak)
   dominant.
Fraxinus excelsior (ash)
   sub-dominant.
Acer campestre (field maple)
   sub-dominant.

Avenues

Quercus robur (oak)
Tilia sp. (lime)
Aesculus hippocastanum (horse chestnut)
   environs of villages only.
Avenues – all as single species, not mixed.

Stream sides, wet clay soils

Alnus glutinosa (alder)
   dominant, in copses, small groups and
   river banks.
Salix alba (white willow)
   sub-dominant; not in mixes.
Salix fragilis (crack willow)
   forms typical pollarded trees, also river
   banks.
Salix caprea (goat willow)
   scrubby copses.
Fraxinus excelsior (ash)
   occasional where not waterlogged.
Quercus robur (oak)
   occasional where not waterlogged.
Corylus avellana (hazel)
   occasional on stream banks if not
   waterlogged.
Populus tremula (aspen)
   in thickets; not in mixes.
Viburnum opulus (guelder rose)
   occasional as individuals and small
   groups.
Cornus sanguinea (dogwood)
   occasional as individuals and small
   groups.

AREA 6: NENE VALLEY/ PETERBOROUGH GRAVELS

Like the Ouse Valley, this was an important area for early settlement, reaching national significance in the Roman period when Durobrivae was a major town on Ermine St, surrounded by pottery kilns that produced distinctive fine and coarse wares for a large part of eastern England. Prehistoric settlements and religious sites were particularly important in the area of Maxey, Etton and Bainton.

The character of the Nene Valley changes greatly as it moves from the shallow undulations of the clay/limestone junction west of Peterborough to the flatter fen edge to the east.

Ferry Meadows Country Park and associated recreational facilities, such as the Nene Valley Railway, dominate the western portion of this area. The intensive, organised landscape around the lakes gradually changes to a pastoral agricultural use that still retains extensive areas of flood meadows and associated sites of nature conservation interest.

Generally, field patterns are still evident with a fairly good cover of hedgerows and trees. Riverside vegetation of trees, and diverse marginal and aquatic plants are to be found in several locations, especially among the backwaters.

East of Peterborough the landform flattens and the river has been adapted to the rectilinear drainage pattern of the fens. The recent excavations at Flag Fen indicate the former importance of this area. The old course of the River Nene meanders south to disappear in a series of small drains around Farcet, whereas the new cut taking the river heads directly east across

Nene Valley: Stibbington.

the fens. This fen edge landscape consists of large open arable fields with sparse tree cover. The tall chimneys of the brickworks based around the clay pits at Whittlesey and south of Peterborough punctuate the skyline.

PRINCIPLES FOR LANDSCAPE IMPROVEMENT AND MANAGEMENT IN THE NENE VALLEY/PETERBOROUGH GRAVELS AREA

The aim should be to strengthen the distinct landscape characteristics of the River Nene either side of Peterborough.

To the east, the open fenland character should dominate.

1. Management of the wetlands in and around the Nene Washes: the Nene Washes are widely recognised for their nature conservation importance. Low-

key alterations to surrounding dykes and their margins would be beneficial to the appearance of the local landscape and nature conservation.

2. Planting around settlement edges: the fringes of settlements would be greatly enhanced by the planting of woodland belts to provide shelter and screening to reduce the impact of their stark and often unattractive visual appearance.

3. Pollarded willows: some dyke-sides are characterised by rows of old pollarded willows. A management cycle for repollarding those still remaining would help to retain these as a feature. A few, carefully chosen sites could be planted with new willows to be pollarded to maintain the continuity of this characteristic feature.

West of Peterborough, the Nene Valley has an important recreational role. A successful planned landscape has been established near the New Town. The extension of this further west is proposed and should include the following:

1. **Management of existing woods:** this will ensure the long-term survival of important landscape features, such as the woods which form the backdrop to Ferry Meadows Country Park.

2. **Creation of small copses:** associated with footpaths or the meandering river, these would add character and interest as well as having wildlife value.

3. **River corridor improvements:** a range of opportunities exist to improve and diversify the margins of the River Nene. These include riverside tree planting and habitat improvements such as creating seasonal wetlands, on-stream slack water areas, off-stream ponds and establishment of appropriate marginal and aquatic plants (see Farmland Model A6 on p. 38). Initially this could concentrate on the low-key waterside recreational areas at Alwalton, Water Newton and Stibbington.

4. **Railway corridor improvements:** landscape improvements to create selected vistas or viewpoints by hedge, tree and copse planting would improve the attractiveness of the Nene Valley Steam Railway.

5. **Footpath corridor improvements:** the Nene Way is a popular recreational route. Features integrated with 3 and 4 above would produce a co-ordinated programme that could significantly improve the quality of the Nene Valley (see Farmland Model A7 on p. 39).

PLANT SPECIES FOR THE NENE VALLEY/PETERBOROUGH GRAVELS AREA
Clay soils (except valley bottoms and wet sites)

Mixed woodlands
Quercus robur (oak)
  dominant tree.
Fraxinus excelsior (ash)
  dominant tree.
Prunus avium (wild cherry)
  less common.
Acer campestre (field maple)
  glades, near edges.
Corylus avellana (hazel)
  dominant shrub, edges, glades, scrub.
Crataegus monogyna (hawthorn)
  near edges, mixed thickets.
Sambucus nigra (elder)
  occasional, understorey and edges.

Hedgerows, woodland edges and scrub
Crataegus monogyna (hawthorn)
Corylus avellana (hazel)
Prunus spinosa (blackthorn)
Rosa canina (dog rose)
Acer campestre (field maple)
Malus sylvestris (crab apple)
Cornus sanguinea (dogwood)
  occasional.

Trees in hedgerows
Quercus robur (oak)
  dominant.
Fraxinus excelsior (ash)
  sub-dominant.
Acer campestre (field maple)
  sub-dominant.

Avenues
Quercus robur (oak)
Tilia sp. (lime)
Aesculus hippocastanum (horse chestnut)
  environs of villages only.
Avenues – all as single species, not mixed.

Stream sides, wet clay soils

Alnus glutinosa (alder)
   dominant, in copses, small groups and
   river banks.

Salix alba (white willow)
   sub-dominant, not in mixes.

Salix fragilis (crack willow)
   forms typical pollarded trees, also river
   banks.

Salix caprea (goat willow)
   scrubby copses.

Fraxinus excelsior (ash)
   occasional where not waterlogged.

Quercus robur (oak)
   occasional where not waterlogged.

Corylus avellana (hazel)
   occasional on stream banks if not
   waterlogged.

Populus tremula (aspen)
   in thickets, not in mixes.

Viburnum opulus (guelder rose)
   occasional as individuals and small
   groups.

Cornus sanguinea (dogwood)
   occasional as individuals and small
   groups.

Gravel soils

Alnus glutinosa (alder)
   dominant, copses, small groups, river
   banks.

Populus alba (white poplar)
   occasional, individuals, small groups.

Populus canescens (grey poplar)
   occasional, individuals, small thickets.

Salix caprea (goat willow)
   scrub, thickets, not mixed.

Salix alba (white willow)
   sub-dominant, not in mixes.

Quercus robur (oak)
   occasional, drier conditions, hedgerows,
   woodlands.

Fraxinus excelsior (ash)
   occasional, drier conditions, hedgerows,
   woodlands.

AREA 7: NORTH-WEST LIMESTONE

This compact area, a remnant of the former Rockingham Forest, has a distinct character that is typical of much of Northamptonshire rather than Cambridgeshire. It has fine landscape qualities which need careful management and selective improvements. Small villages with buildings constructed in local limestone, many with Collyweston slate roofs, are located in these low limestone hills. Mixed farming still occurs in the area, so the traditional pattern of fields enclosed by hedges or drystone walls is characteristic. Arable fields tend to be larger, and many of the hedgerows have been removed. Here the landscape can nevertheless be attractive with the large rolling fields flowing between significant woods and small copses, which provide a sense of enclosure and also frame long-distance views. There are some fine ancient semi-natural woodlands and other woods are valuable sites of nature conservation interest. A number of relic floral grassland sites, including some road verges, are also of significance. Barnack Hills and Holes and Castor Hanglands are particularly fine landscape sites with considerable nature conservation value.

PRINCIPLES FOR LANDSCAPE IMPROVEMENT AND MANAGEMENT IN THE NORTH-WEST LIMESTONE AREA

Essentially the aim is to achieve contrasts between areas of small-scale intimate landscape character full of detail and interest, and open fields sweeping amongst and enclosed by bold masses of woodlands. In the future, a greater sense of enclosure

North-west Limestone: west of Peterborough.

should be developed by careful woodland planting and management. Within this framework, detailed restoration and habitat creation projects relating to drystone walls and flower-rich road verges, for example, can be carried out.

1. **Management of existing woodlands:** this should aim to achieve the progressive conversion of conifer plantations to mixed broad-leaved woodlands where possible and the careful management of ancient semi-natural woodlands and re-stocking, coppicing and creation of 'edge areas' elsewhere (see Farmland Model A4b on p. 36).

2. **Road margins:** the repair of drystone walls, replanting of hedges with trees and management of verges for floral diversity would help retain or restore some of the small-scale, intimate nature of this area which has been degraded by the loss of field hedgerows.

3. **Drystone walls:** a maintenance programme is essential; new walls should be built in the traditional pattern where possible.

4. **Hedgerows:** selected hedgerows should be reinforced or managed for particularly significant impact, based upon their visual and wildlife potential. Historically significant hedgerows should be carefully conserved, and new hedges planted to emphasise the existing landscape.

5. **Footpath corridor improvements:** a number of footpaths in the area have been improved by waymarking and the construction of stiles and footbridges. The next stage is to enhance the experience of walking through this landscape by the creation of features of interest, vistas and viewpoints along the key footpath corridors (see Farmland Model A7 on p. 39).

6. Planting a few carefully located woodland belts: linking woodland blocks and aligned to reinforce landforms, the woodland belts would enclose open, rolling areas of farmland and enhance significant views. If suitably sited, these may help to reduce the visual dominance of the electricity transmission lines which bisect the area.

7. Villages: most villages are attractive and have, generally, been protected from unsympathetic peripheral development. The villages are an integral part of the landscape and often combine successfully with it. Attention

NORTH-WEST LIMESTONE Before

Loss of hedgerows.   Poor health of hedgerow trees.   Significant woods and copses give good enclosure to broad views.

NORTH-WEST LIMESTONE After

Hedgerows replanted along road sides.   Verges managed for grass and floral diversity.   New woodlands to improve sense of scale and enclose rolling landform.

should be focused on improvements to village entrances, and tree and hedge planting to subdue the visual dominance of overhead wires and screen views into the rear of properties. Ensure that key features such as avenues at Southorpe, or views to prominent landmarks such as church towers, are not lost.

8. Grasslands: some of the thinner limestone soils give marginal yields for arable crops in dry years, creating the potential to transfer them to grassland. The species-rich meadows at Barnack Hills and Holes and the superb Castor Hanglands illustrate the potential for achieving particularly fine landscape, including species-rich grassland, on limestone soils.

PLANT SPECIES GUIDELINES FOR THE NORTH-WEST LIMESTONE AREA

Mixed woodlands

Fraxinus excelsior (ash)
  dominant tree.
Quercus robur (oak)
  on deeper soils.
Prunus avium (wild cherry)
Acer campestre (field maple)
  glades, near edges.
Corylus avellana (hazel)
  main understorey shrub, glades and thickets.
Crataegus monogyna (hawthorn)
  near edges, thickets.
Sambucus nigra (elder)
  occasional, understorey and edges.

Hedgerows, woodland edges and scrub

Crataegus monogyna (hawthorn)
Corylus avellana (hazel)
Prunus spinosa (blackthorn)
Acer campestre (field maple)
Rosa canina (dog rose)
Malus sylvestris (crab apple)

Trees in hedgerows

Fraxinus excelsior (ash)
  dominant.
Quercus robur (oak)
  deeper soils only.
Acer campestre (field maple)
Malus sylvestris (crab apple)

Avenues/village approaches

Quercus robur (oak)
Aesculus hippocastanum (horse chestnut)
Tilia sp. (lime)
Avenues – all as single species, not mixed.

AREA 8: FENLAND

HISTORICAL DEVELOPMENT

The fens are a complex landscape covering 550 sq. miles produced from draining the tidal basin of the Wash. The area has undergone continual transformation since the last ice age 10,000 years ago, as with each relative change in sea level the balance between saltmarsh, fen, bog and woodland has altered. Large-scale drainage work in the Fenland stems from the human desire to manage these potentially productive lands. This has been achieved in three principal phases spanning the last 2,000 years.

1. The silty marine deposits lying around the Wash became habitable for the first time during the Roman period with the construction of a sea wall around the Wash to exclude the

Fenland: 16-ft drain at Stonea.

highest tides. The nature of the settlement was rural with farms clinging to the higher ground along the levees of streams and rivers. The main economic activities were salt production, using fen peat and the tidal salt water in the brooks, and the rearing of sheep and cattle. Various canals were made, mainly for transport, linking major rivers, or, like the Fen Causeway, connecting the Peterborough region with East Anglia. This canal became silted and was later turned into a road. An even longer waterway, the Car Dyke, linked Lincoln with Peterborough from where connection with Cambridge could be made via natural rivers and finally by the Cambridgeshire Car Dyke cutting through Cottenham and Waterbeach.

2. In the early Middle Ages much of the remaining fenland was drained through 'assarting', the process by which common land is enclosed by private landowners. This produced extensive areas of pasture and the products which formed the basis of the wealthy Fenland economy – meat, butter, wool, livestock and traditional products of reed, sedge and peat.

3. The final major phase of drainage was designed by Vermuyden and implemented in the seventeenth century, with an elaborate system of drains and river diversions, including the construction of the Ouse washes.

This scheme enabled deep drainage of the southern peat fens leading to the conversion of pasture to arable cultivation, which in turn accelerated the shrinkage of peat resulting in the need to maintain most of Fenland by continued pumping into the now higher drainage channels and rivers.

FENLAND ARCHAEOLOGY

Fen islands and edges are exciting archaeological areas because their build-up of peat has protected early sites. Lowest levels are still wet and therefore preserve organic materials and other evidence. The area has always been rich in natural resources (e.g. waterfowl, peat, reed) and was settled wherever changing water levels permitted. Early prehistoric habitation was widespread and the Romans organised drainage and farmed the fens as an imperial estate, probably concentrating on wool and leather production for the army. Saxon monks actually experienced wetter conditions providing them with remote strongholds at Ely, Ramsey and Thorney.

Peat shrinkage is constantly exposing new archaeological sites in the Fenlands, and therefore up-to-date information is always needed before development or planting schemes are planned. Survey work carried out by English Heritage's Fenland Project provides invaluable information for individual sites.

LANDSCAPE CHARACTERISTICS

Fenland is a landscape of contrasts and variety. Superimposed upon the regimented and highly organised drainage patterns is a much more haphazard pattern of settlement and tree cover. It is a large open landscape and although appearing monotonous, it is in fact characterised by continuous change as the visual characteristics of one fen merge into the next. The open landscape provides distant views where the scattering of clumps and individual trees merge together to produce a feeling of a more densely tree-covered horizon.

There are many 'islands' which rise above the flat ocean of the fens. These range in size from the dominant Isle of Ely which rises over 20m above the adjacent peat fens, to much smaller features which are elevated an almost imperceptible metre or two. These islands are significant in the

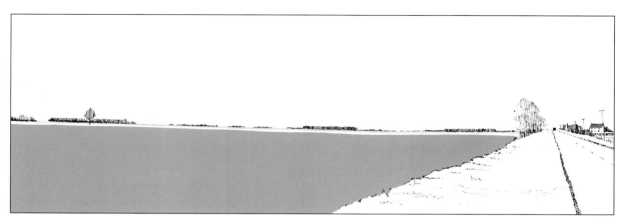

Wide open spaces; distant trees merge to form a softened horizon, but uncluttered spaces of several square miles in extent create a dramatic and dominant character.

landscape: most are occupied by settlements or farmsteads which, with their associated tree cover, gives them special prominence. Heavier soils predominate on the larger islands, resulting in a landscape more typical of the Western Claylands with mature trees and thick hedgerows.

In the expansive open landscape isolated agricultural buildings, farmsteads and loose-knit villages are often prominent against a background of a constantly changing sky where vast cloudscapes provide drama and visual delight.

There is considerable variation within Fenland, each fen having its own characteristics. Journeying through Fenland these subtle changes in character become gradually apparent with the constant change in the balance of landscape components.

Examples of areas within Fenland with strong individual characteristics include:
– the larger islands of higher ground such as at March, Chatteris, Haddenham and Ely. These have more tree cover, retained hedgerows and often extensive areas of grassland;
– the Duke of Bedford's former estate at Thorney where nineteenth-century planting on a grand scale has produced a landscape strongly influenced by tree belts and avenues;
– the fruit-growing area around Wisbech including villages such as Parson Drove, Wisbech St Mary and Leverington, situated on the northern silt fens. Here an early settlement pattern with an irregular layout of connecting roads combines with mature trees in the villages and orchards surrounded by windbreaks of poplar or hawthorn to produce a

distinctive landscape;
– land adjacent to the Ouse and Nene Washes, and other large drainage channels where huge linear grassy banks dominate the landscape;
– extensive plantations of poplar in the Shippea Hill area, once grown for match production, have produced blocks of woodland in scale with the open landscape;
– extensive linear planting of poplars and willow on field edges and road verges in the Isleham–Prickwillow area on the initiative of vegetable growers has produced features which now dominate the local landscape;
– remnant wet fenlands at Wicken, Holme and Woodwalton dominate the local landscapes and provide a sharp contrast with modern usage of the fens.

PRINCIPLES FOR LANDSCAPE IMPROVEMENT AND MANAGEMENT IN THE FENLAND AREA

The fens are large open landscapes. Their present character is a result of the interrelation between the regimented pattern of drains and roads and the more scattered elements of trees and settlements. In many areas the essential character is the open view of land, sky and the field drains. Any landscape proposal must suit the massive scale of the landscape and be in keeping with the local character of the particular area.

Tree and Hedge Planting
1. **Around agricultural buildings and farmsteads:** modern farm operations require large, industrially scaled buildings. The scale of the fen landscape can enable these to become

FENLAND Before

Wide sweeping vistas where the farm buildings are the main element to break the skyline.

FENLAND After

Planting concentrated around the farmhouse and its 'industrial' scale buildings. This would provide shelter and soften the forms of the buildings.

No planting along drove because this would conflict with the wide open vista.

Encourage verge and dykeside vegetation for wildlife.

an acceptable element in distant views. Careful siting and choice of colour cladding is important. Attempts at screening need to be equally bold to succeed. However, it is not necessary to surround buildings with trees. Planting of up to quarter of a hectare of trees in front, to the side or even behind buildings will soften the harsh outlines of buildings and combine to form visual 'islands' within the open Fenland.

2. Isolated trees and clumps: a characteristic feature of Fenland is the scattering of lone trees, often willows of pollarded origin, which grow on drove edges, road verges, out of ditch banks or adjacent to buildings. Small-scale planting is needed if the presence of isolated mature trees is to be maintained in the landscape. The regular shape of fen fields and the large number of drains provide few obvious sites for planting even occasional trees. A willingness to tolerate 'lone' trees in an arable environment will be needed by farmers and landowners, to perpetuate their presence in Fenland.

3. Planting of avenues/tree belts: the planting of avenues and lines of trees can do much to improve and diversify the landscape if undertaken on an appropriate scale. The tree belts in the Thorney area are appropriate because they were planted on a grand scale by the Duke of Bedford and in combination they produce the character of that area. An isolated avenue or tree belt is likely to appear out of place on its own, within an open landscape.

The planting of avenues/tree belts should be undertaken:
– within areas already characterised by similar features;
– where the scale of work is appropriately large, e.g. as part of a planned scheme covering a large estate;
– after consideration has been paid to the qualities of the existing landscape and the impact of the belts on existing views, e.g. will an existing prominent view of Ely Cathedral be lost?

4. Planting of new woodlands: true woodland is largely absent from Fenland, though records show that

FENLAND Before

FENLAND After

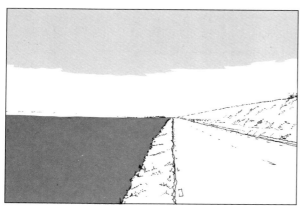

FENLAND Village Entrance: Before

FENLAND Village Entrance: After

some ancient woodland did survive on the larger fen islands until quite recent times, the last site being cleared at Doddington earlier this century. It is on these larger islands that new woodland planting would be most appropriate. For example, there could be substantial benefits from establishing extensive new woodlands on the fen islands around Ely, Chatteris and March.

5. Settlements and large developments: many Fenland villages have suffered from unsightly fringe development. Planting thick hedgerows with trees or wider shelterbelts on the margins would soften harsh boundaries between rear gardens and farmland. These types of landscaping opportunities should be incorporated into sizeable developments affecting the edges of settlements. Entrances to

Fenland: the Isle of Ely from Stuntney.

some villages would be improved by tree planting along verges. Avenue planting of large trees with scale and presence, such as horse chestnut, is appropriate. Tree planting within the settlements will soften their profiles and reinforce their island character within the open fen setting.

6. Fen islands: opportunities should be sought to increase tree cover through hedgerow planting, and the creation of new copses and woodland, thus providing a contrast to the surrounding fens. At the transition area between fen and island, the creation of small grass paddocks surrounded with thick hedges and trees or areas of woodland would reinforce the contrast and the sense of moving from one landscape to another.

Management of Dykes and Drains

In managing these features opportunities should be taken to enhance the landscape and conservation value by:
– reprofiling banks;
– creating dyke deltas;
– encouraging more diverse grass and flora species by extending clearance cycles.

Recreating Wet Fenland

In the intensively managed fenland landscape few areas of semi-natural fenland remain. All practical opportunities for recreating wet fenland should be exploited.

PLANT SPECIES GUIDELINES FOR FENLAND

Since many of Fenland's trees are of planted origin we will find that the typical naturally occurring species such as willow, ash, oak and elm are very commonly supplemented with introduced horse chestnut and sycamore. As a general rule these should only be used in villages or in association with buildings.

Peat and silt Fenland

Fraxinus excelsior (ash)

Salix alba (white willow)

Alnus glutinosa (alder)

Quercus robur (oak)

Acer campestre (field maple)

Betula pendula (birch)

Populus alba (white poplar)

Populus robusta (hybrid black poplar)

Salix caprea (goat willow)

Salix cinerea (grey willow)

Crataegus monogyna (hawthorn)

Viburnum opulus (guelder rose)

Cornus sanguinea (dogwood)

Aesculus hippocastanum (horse chestnut)

Acer pseudoplatanus (sycamore)

Fen islands

Fraxinus excelsior (ash)

Quercus robur (oak)

Acer campestre (field maple)

Malus sylvestris (crab apple)

Prunus avium (wild cherry)

Salix alba (white willow)

Salix caprea (goat willow)

Crataegus monogyna (hawthorn)

Corylus avellana (hazel)

Cornus sanguinea (dogwood)

Prunus spinosa (blackthorn)

Ligustrum vulgare (wild privet)

Selected dykes could form linear landscape corridors through the fens. Here, a smaller-scale character is appropriate, with meadows, copses, pollarded willows, changes of level and wetland habitats. From these more sheltered corridors, there would be contrasting views out to the open Fenland beyond.

5

**MAKE
IT
HAPPEN**

DEVELOPERS, LANDOWNERS, LAND MANAGERS, FARMERS, VOLUNTEERS

When it comes to action to safeguard or improve the landscape, you are in the front line. You are expected to follow the guidelines in this manual. When all do so, we shall witness the much needed transformation of the Cambridgeshire landscape.

There may be help available, should you need it, from the local authorities or from a variety of other sources (see pp. 83–6).

Please bear in mind the need for major imaginative projects which may be promoted by the local authorities and government agencies and help if you can. For example:

– **New Cambridgeshire forests:** these would consist of multi-purpose woodland blocks interspersed with farmland, as described in the Rural Strategy. Possible locations are on the Chalklands south-east of Cambridge, the Western Claylands to the west of the A1, or to the south and west of Peterborough.

– **Major countryside routes:** the County and District Councils have promoted several medium- to long-distance paths which include the Roman Road, Wimpole Way, Ouse Valley Way and Hereward Way. These routes often follow historic trackways, link features of interest and cross a variety of landscape characters. They could be much enhanced through landscape renewal within their visual corridor, by creating new green lanes, hedges, small-scale habitat improvements and features such as 'landmark' copses and avenues.

– **Chalk grassland:** at one time, the chalklands were extensively covered by grassland with sheep grazing, a management regime which led to floristically very diverse and attractive meadows. These are now largely lost due to conversion to intensive arable production. The Institute of Terrestrial Ecology has been conducting trials near Royston over some years to assess the feasibility of restoring the chalkland meadows and thus a 'downs' character. It is proposed that an extensive area be transformed back to a traditional chalk grassland, with the help of ITE's experience, with the objective of associated public access, environmental education use and wildlife conservation.

– **Arboretum:** it is envisaged that an arboretum could help revitalise an existing woodland or parkland estate and form a natural extension to it. Some of the benefits would be: to enhance the present range of public open space facilities; to provide a series of walks or trails through a variety of landscapes; to provide a source of educational or scientific studies; and to create a new landscape feature adding to the richness of Cambridgeshire's environment.

LOCAL AUTHORITIES

The county, district and parish councils of Cambridgeshire have a vital role to play in the implementation of these guidelines through:

– policy guidance;
– planning control;
– education and publicity;
– guardianship;
– direct action.

ACTION THROUGH POLICY GUIDANCE

In addition to this manual there is a range of planning and other rural policy documents which include guidance on landscape issues:

    – County Structure Plan;
    – District Local Plans;
    – Aggregates Local Plan;
    – Cambridge Green Belt Local Plan;
    – Ouse Valley Recreation Local Plan;
    – Cambridgeshire Rural Strategy.

When these documents are reviewed, the effectiveness of the policies should be assessed in terms of the landscape guidelines, in particular to establish whether sufficient emphasis is placed on creative policies and the need to develop landscape character and a sense of place.

INFLUENCE THROUGH PLANNING CONTROL

The county and district councils have considerable influence through the planning system over development within and adjoining the countryside, although there are significant exclusions (such as small farm buildings and forestry). In addition, their powers are clearly limited by statute and may be overturned on appeal.

Nevertheless, the planning system should be used to reinforce the principles contained within these guidelines. In particular, planners are encouraged to:
– be positive in encouraging development which, provided it is acceptable in broad planning terms, offers a creative response to change in the countryside and also environmentally based 'planning gain';
– place greater emphasis, at an earlier stage, on requiring landscape assessments or (for larger or more sensitive developments) environmental statements to be prepared;
– require developers and others who submit proposals to show not only how impact on the countryside is minimised but also how the development can contribute to the richness, diversity and character of the area; use Tree Preservation Orders to safeguard existing trees and ensure through planning conditions that landscape proposals are properly carried out;
– expect all significant proposals to be supported by a landscape response which has been properly prepared by a qualified landscape architect or other discipline as appropriate;
– maintain a dialogue with developers to discuss how best the principles contained in these guidelines can be achieved;
– ensure that the planning control system is properly supported by professional landscape advice, either by appointing one or more landscape architects to their staff or by using consultants to assist 'as required'.

INFLUENCE THROUGH EDUCATION AND PUBLICITY

Through environmental education in schools, a new generation of children can grow up with a better understanding of their environment and their relationship to it; in particular, they should be encouraged to understand that the environment is not a vague concept and something that only happens elsewhere, in the Amazon jungle or the upper atmosphere, or that it is entirely outside their control as individuals, but is as much as anything their local landscape – town, village and countryside. Through this appreciation, children can be encouraged to take an active role in caring for the countryside and helping to implement some of the proposals contained in these guidelines.

For the general public, leaflets, booklets, exhibitions and television programmes are important media in helping to open eyes to countryside issues. Through interpretive programmes, people can understand the forces which shape the countryside, form views on priorities and future directions and, perhaps, actively contribute to improving landscape quality through their own activities and influence on others.

ACTION THROUGH GUARDIANSHIP

Parish councils are best placed to know which landscape features are valued by their local communities. Local concern, and the action which flows from it, is one of the best ways of ensuring the protection and conservation of locally cherished landscapes.

DIRECT ACTION

Local authorities can take a leading role in promoting action to conserve and improve the landscape. Owing to limitations on staff time and resources, local authorities often work most effectively as 'enablers' by:

    – supporting and encouraging the voluntary section, e.g. with grant aid;
– providing advice and support for the many private landowners and farmers who wish to act as custodians of the countryside;
– raising the level of public knowledge and appreciation of the landscape, thus building motivation for action.

Local authorities may also engage in direct action through landscape improvement on their own land (where they may be setting an important example as on the County Farms Estate) or by working in co-operation with others. They can plug into the large network of organisations (national and local; official and private) who share concern for our landscape heritage. By this means far more can be achieved than if each organisation works to its own objectives dependent on its own resources. The Rural Strategy provides the framework for this, and examples of effective joint projects include the Peterborough, Ouse Valley and Cambridge Green Belt countryside management projects.

Local authorities should:
– review the policy framework and consider whether sufficient emphasis has been placed on the need to develop landscape character and a sense of place;
– use the planning system creatively to reinforce the principles of the guidelines;
– review their commitment to environmental education and interpretation, as it is through information and understanding about the countryside that care and concern is engendered;

– encourage local communities to identify the special features of their local landscapes and take action to conserve them;

– review, and if possible strengthen, their role as grant-aiding and enabling organisations to promote more action on the ground;

– review their commitment to landscape improvement in the countryside on landholdings where they have direct control – this will include land in various local authority departments such as Education, Transportation and Recreation;

– be prepared to research and promote major new landscape initiatives in conjunction with other interested organisations.

SOURCES OF ADVICE AND GRANT AID

LOCAL AUTHORITIES

Cambridgeshire County Council
Rural Group
Shire Hall
Castle Hill
Cambridge CB3 0AP
Tel: Cambridge 0223-317404

- Advice on all aspects of countryside management
- Grant aid
- Register of archaeological sites

East Cambridgeshire District Council
The Grange
Nutholt Lane
Ely
Cambs CB7 4PL
Tel: Ely 0353-665555

- Planning and arboricultural advice

Fenland District Council
Fenland Hall
County Road
March
Cambs PE15 8NQ
Tel: March 0354-54321

- Planning and arboricultural advice

Huntingdonshire District Council
Pathfinder House
St Mary's Street
Huntingdon
Cambs PE18 6TN
Tel: Huntingdon 0480-456161

- Planning and arboricultural advice
- Grants for small tree planting schemes
- Ouse Valley Countryside Management Project – advice and grants for small improvement works

Peterborough City Council
Town Hall
Bridge Street
Peterborough
Cambs PE1 1HG
Tel: Peterborough 0733-63141

- Planning and arboricultural advice
- Peterborough Countryside Management Project – advice and grants for small improvement works

South Cambridgeshire District Council
9–11 Hills Road
Cambridge CB2 1PB
Tel: Cambridge 0223-351795

- Planning, conservation and arboricultural advice
- Grants for tree planting and surgery in villages

Cambridge City Council
The Guildhall
Cambridge CB2 3QD
Tel: Cambridge 0223-358977

- Planning and arboricultural advice

COUNTRYSIDE COMMISSION

Countryside Commission
(Eastern Region)
Ortona House
110 Hills Road
Cambridge CB2 1NL
Tel: Cambridge 0223-354462

- Promotion of countryside conservation
- Advice and grant aid for a range of landscape and countryside conservation initiatives

FORESTRY COMMISSION

Forestry Commission
Great Eastern House
Tenison Road
Cambridge CB1 2DU
Tel: Cambridge 0223-314546

- Advice on commercial management and new planting through the Commission's grant schemes

MINISTRY OF AGRICULTURE

MAFF Grants Section
Chequers Court
Huntingdon
Cambs PE18 6LT
Tel: Huntingdon 0480-52161

- Grants for woodlands and conservation management on the farm

ADAS
Chequers Court
Huntingdon
Cambs PE18 6LT
Tel: Huntingdon 0480-52161

- Agricultural advisory service including conservation advice

FWAG
Farming & Wildlife Advisory Group
Anstey Hall
Maris Lane
Trumpington
Cambridge CB2 2LS
Tel: Cambridge 0223-840011

- Whole farm conservation advice and evaluation of conservation features

WILDLIFE TRUSTS
The Wildlife Trust of Bedfordshire & Cambridgeshire
5 Fulbourn Manor
Fulbourn
Cambridge CB1 5BN
Tel: Cambridge 0223-8800788

- Survey and advice on management of wildlife sites

Northamptonshire Wildlife Trust
Lings House
Billing Lings
Northampton NN3 4BE
Tel: Northampton 0604-405285

- Survey and advice on management of wildlife sites in the Peterborough area

ENGLISH NATURE
(previously Nature Conservancy Council)
Eastern Region
English Nature
Northminster House
Peterborough PE1 1UA
Tel: Peterborough 0733-340345

- Nature conservation advice and grant aid
- Advice on management of 'statutory' wildlife sites

LANDSCAPE ARCHITECTS
Landscape Institute
12 Carlton House Terrace
London SW1Y 4AH
Tel: 071-839 4044

- Landscape advice
- List of landscape architects

CHARTERED SURVEYORS
Royal Institution of Chartered Surveyors
12 Great George Street
Parliament Square
London SW1P 3AD
Tel: 071-222 7000

- Land agency advice
- List of chartered surveyors

CHARTERED FORESTERS

Institute of Chartered Foresters
22 Walker Street
Edinburgh EH3 7HR
Tel: 031-2252705

- Advice on commercial forestry
- List of consultants